WHAT READE]

C000182169

"Perrine is an inspirational lead‹
value what we have in commo.
differences, open and inclusive to all, offering personal and company growth."

John Finney
CEO, Isotropic

Whenever I am asked "What makes the most successful startups?" my answer is always "the team." It is proven that the most successful teams are ones with diverse perspectives and background. This must-read book will challenge you to think not only about the value of diversity and inclusion in your business, but more importantly, practical steps that you can take on creating a truly inclusive and more successful business.

Andrew Macadam
Global Field Lead, Microsoft for Startups

"Building an inclusive workplace can supercharge your organisation. And Perrine Farque's *INCLUSION* is the guide you need to make that happen. Packed with insight and inspiration, as well as powerful tips and tools, this book is a godsend for any organisation seeking to tap the many benefits of a more diverse workforce."

Carl Honoré
Author of *Bolder: Making The Most Of Our Longer Lives*

Equality is a foundation designed to create a more level playing field where all have an equal advantage to strive. This book brings together a wealth of experience to provide a comprehensive and highly accessible practical guide for leaders, managers, HR and diversity and inclusion professionals to create genuine inclusion and belonging throughout an organisation. Perrine tackles this complex and often misunderstood topic on a very human level, providing background and theory before considering what they mean for you and me and how to act upon them to affect change. It's a must-read for anyone wanting to make meaningful, tangible and sustainable long-term change in the workplace.

Cheryl Cole
Editor, DiversityQ.com

INCLUSION: The Ultimate Secret for an Organization's Success, written by Perrine Farque, not only succinctly articulates why leaders should prioritise inclusion, but also provides expert guidance on how to create inclusive leaders and environments for both office and remote workers. After all, only inclusive leaders can effectively create that culture of inclusion and belonging that organisations are so desperately seeking right now, because, ultimately, it's key to their future survival and success. This book is full of case studies to showcase what inclusion and inclusive leaders look like. It's also packed with practical tips and pointers on how to avoid the many pitfalls. Thanks to her diversity and inclusion expertise, Perrine provides powerful and inspiring insights to help hone your inclusion knowledge and skills. As she aptly points out: "Just one act of inclusion is capable of changing your day, your team, and maybe your entire organisation." In short, a must-read for all 'wannabe' inclusive leaders and managers.

Pepi Sappal
Director & Founder, Fair Play Talks

Issues around diversity and inclusion finally have the societal platform they deserve, but tangible progress in the workplace still leaves much to be desired. With the world's eyes watching, the onus is now on business leaders to ensure these principles sit at the core of company strategy, particularly when remote working makes cultural cohesion so difficult to nurture. Although many leaders understand that inclusion is important and enhances team performance, implementing this organically is another matter altogether. This book provides invaluable, practical guidance for how to grow an organisation by fostering an environment that is inclusive and democratic.

Russ Shaw CBE
Founder
Tech London Advocates & Global Tech Advocates

INCLUSION: The Ultimate Secret for an Organization's Success is a must-read for any professional who wants to become the inclusive leader they always aspired to be. This book provides practical and actionable steps to lead by including everyone and it defines the positive impact inclusion has on an organization's performance. Perrine Farque has written a must-read for anyone considering becoming a better leader...Read this book and learn from one of the best.

Jamie Turner
Author, Professor, Consultant

Farque insights help us overcome our deepest fears of being excluded or discarded, allowing us to feel truly appreciated and loved for our true selves. Which, allows us to do the same for others.

Erik Qualman
#1 Bestselling Author of *Socialnomics*

Perrine Farque is a champion on DEI issues, and I have worked closely with her to train our leaders and employees at Salary Finance. When we listen and celebrate what is both common and different, we become wiser, more inclusive, and better as a fintech firm with a social purpose to make millions of lives healthier and happier. We are building products that people with very diverse backgrounds use, and I think we all want our company makeup to reflect the makeup of the people who use our products.

Daniel Shakhani
Co-founder, Salary Finance

"Inclusivity is now undeniably a critical success factor—its presence will mark out those businesses that succeed and those that fail in the post-Covid world. If there's someone out there who understands this urgent new agenda and its demands and dynamics better than Perrine Farque, then I've yet to meet them. In this book, she clearly, succinctly and unjudgementally unpacks what successful inclusivity looks like, and how it can be attained. If you want to remain, or aspire to become, a successful leader, this is a must-read book."

Joel Harrison
Co-founder and Editor-in-chief
B2B Marketing

"Creating an inclusive and supportive workplace is the cornerstone of building sustainably successful businesses. Perrine Farque takes us through the fundamentals that are helpful for anyone looking to develop inclusiveness in their business, and especially for business leaders who wish not only to create financial success but also to recruit and retain the best talent."

Amali Alwis, MD
Microsoft for Startups UK

INCLUSION

INCLUSION

THE ULTIMATE SECRET FOR

AN ORGANIZATION'S SUCCESS

Perrine Farque

• WRITE WAY •
PUBLISHING COMPANY
RALEIGH, NORTH CAROLINA

Printed in the United States of America

ISBN 978-1-946425-83-6 softcover
ISBN 978-1-946425-84-3 ebook

Book Design by CSinclaire Write-Design
Cover Design by Klevur

• WRITE WAY •
PUBLISHING COMPANY
RALEIGH, NORTH CAROLINA

For Matteo Frigeri, the calming force
behind my relentless energy.

For our children, Manuel and Victoria,
who inspire me every day to build a better world.

For our parents, who always believed in us,
and for my siblings Alix-Anne and Victor
who have always been here for us.

CONTENT

FOREWORD

Creating an inclusive and collaborative work environment has always been something that is important to me. In 2020, the FinTech start-up I co-founded and led (Salary Finance) acquired a competitor and overnight we doubled in size to 200+ people in 3 countries. We could no longer rely on culture being developed organically and had to consciously design and build a culture that would deliver on one of our key objectives: to be a great place for every team member to be and grow.

We looked for help to create a truly inclusive, collaborative work environment, and we chose to work with Perrine Farque and her company Inspired Human.

Perrine's work transformed how we approach the diversity and inclusion parts of our culture. Her contribution educated and inspired us to embrace the opportunities that diversity and inclusion present for us as a company, and most importantly, help our colleagues be happy and the best versions of themselves at work.

Perrine's work with us reduced the fear of saying or doing the wrong thing because we built a safe work atmosphere for all, even building our own terminology that everyone understands. Her approach offers a fresh perspective, new ideas, a warm and energetic way to discuss important work on culture issues, and she delivers in an inspirational and passionate style, which made, and continues to make, it very enjoyable to work with her!

And now, in this book, Perrine shares her experience and wisdom on the power—because it is indeed powerful—of inclusion in the workplace. Inclusion - the Secret for an Organization's Success will help business leaders, team leaders, HR professionals, and entrepreneurs understand the impact inclusion has on an organization's performance. Her book also provides very practical and helpful tips gained through her work with local, national, and global brands for conducting successful unconscious bias and diversity and inclusion training, and it clearly articulates why every organization should prioritize inclusion. Perrine's important work brings a powerful perspective to what leadership should look like in today's world: inclusive. Every business leader, entrepreneur, HR professional, and anyone interested in becoming a better leader should read this book!

Asesh Sarkar
Global CEO and Co-founder
Salary Finance

INTRODUCTION

We all share something in common as human beings: a deep desire to belong. We all have that universal need to feel included. From the moment we are born, we naturally look for the connection with other human beings. A newborn baby's bond with its mother is so important in its natural, healthy development. That desire for a deep connection remains true for human beings throughout their life and until they die.

The desire to belong is as necessary to a human being as the need to eat, drink, and have shelter. A human being can't be fulfilled in isolation from his peers. Living in isolation, be it in physical isolation or emotional isolation, has a significant, negative impact on the person's physical, emotional, and mental well-being. The fictional character Robinson Crusoe is a great illustration of a person's most basic need to belong and how living in forced isolation pays its toll on this character's well-being. As the only survivor of a ship wreck, Crusoe notices that he quickly starts to display signs of losing his sanity from the isolation, so he starts writing a journal detailing his daily activities to keep in touch with reality.

Whether we like to admit it or not, we crave that feeling of being loved for who we really are. Deep down, we all want to be seen and loved for ourselves. Our deepest fear is to be rejected, excluded, or discarded. However confident and secure we might look on the outside or even feel on the inside, deep down inside all of us is a strong desire to be accepted and loved for who we truly are. At work, at home, with our friends and family, we want to be seen, accepted, and loved. In every interaction with another human being, we want to be appreciated and valued. Whenever we feel truly appreciated, valued, and loved for our true self, we feel a strong connection with the other person or group, and this opens up all sorts of possibilities. When we feel valued, loved, and accepted, we can take on the impossible. Once that bond is created and nurtured, anything can happen. On the other hand, when we feel like we are not being seen, heard, valued, or loved, a dramatic negative dynamic is created that leads to negative feelings, a lack of trust, and feelings of resentment. Any hope of productive collaboration or creative energy within that relationship is prevented. Whether it's at work, at home, or with friends and family, when someone feels discarded or rejected, they automatically will block any chance of a positive, creative opportunity with that person or group, and that can have devastating consequences.

Considering that inclusion and belonging are the foundation for a strong and cohesive community where every member is thriving, and since most of us spend the majority of our lives at work, the focus of this book will be on inclusion in the workplace. We live in a society that is rapidly changing, where remote work is transforming how people work together. The impact of this rapid change is that employees feel more disconnected, more disengaged, and more isolated from their peers than ever before. The need for connection, belonging, and inclusion is bigger than ever as organizations are adapting to a rapid change in how we work.

In this book, you will learn how to create true inclusion at work, what impact an inclusive workplace has on the organization's performance, who can contribute to creating an inclusive workplace, and, of course, why every organization should prioritize inclusion. You will also learn what inclusion really means, what an inclusive workplace looks like, how an inclusive workplace is the key to creating a successful organization, and how to create an inclusive workplace to fast-track your organizational success.

We all share
something in common
as human beings:
a deep desire
to belong.

1

INCLUSION AND BELONGING

What is inclusion? Inclusion is the feeling of being heard, seen, and valued for who we are. Someone feels included when they feel that they are being seen, heard, valued, respected, and invited by someone or by a group of people. Inclusion is a feeling, not an action. Although there can be acts of inclusion such as inviting someone to a dinner, inviting someone to a meeting, or asking someone what they think about a situation, inclusion comes from a feeling inside a person, a feeling of being welcomed and valued. In fact, it is possible for someone to receive acts of inclusion such as the ones just mentioned, yet not feel included. Inclusion is an emotion felt by someone when they feel they are being seen, heard, and appreciated for who they are.

What is belonging? Belonging is feeling part of a group of people that recognizes us as one of theirs. Belonging is an even stronger connection than inclusion, because it goes beyond feeling included. It is when being part of a group becomes integral to our identity. Belonging means that no matter what, the group will always call us and involve us. Being connected with a group touches each individual's identity.

Inclusion and belonging often go together, but as noted, it is possible to feel included without having the feeling of belonging. It is possible, especially in a workplace environment, that an individual might feel like they are included, in the sense of feeling seen, heard, valued, and respected, yet they might not necessarily feel like they belong to that group of colleagues. They might not feel like that group is part of their identity. On the other hand, when someone feels both included and like they belong to a group at work, this is the ultimate win-win situation for the employee and for the organization. In that case, the individual feels a deep sense of community with the organization, and they feel like being part of the organization is actually part of their identity. Conversely, it is not possible to feel like they belong without feeling included. For someone to feel like they belong to a group, they first must also feel included, meaning they must feel seen, heard, respected, and valued.

In my career as a marketing manager, I never felt like I belonged, and I rarely felt included. Most of the time, I felt like I was not being seen, heard, valued, or respected. For the majority of my career in technology, I felt like my team, my business unit, and the organization did not value me. For example, I was rarely asked for input by my manager, who was my business unit leader. The majority of the time, decisions about the team, the business unit, or the organization were made behind closed doors in the headquarters by a limited group made of senior leaders before being regurgitated to the rest of the organization. I can count on my fingers the number of times I was asked what I thought and what should be done. This lack of inclusion and belonging made me feel very disconnected from my team, from my business unit, and from the organization. It also made me personally question my abilities and had a profound impact on my emotional, mental, and even physical well-being.

However, I had a mentor who was the most inclusive leader I have ever met in my career. Steve was my mentor for several years, and he made me feel not only included but like I belonged in a way no other leader had. By showing up every day and asking me how I was, by always making time for me no matter how busy his day was, by listening to me without interruption, by checking in with me often, Steve acted as an inclusive leader every day. He did this across his team, and therefore, he created a unique inclusive environment around him.

Inclusion and belonging are both universal desires shared by all human beings, and they also are a fundamental part of living well with others, be it at home or in the workplace. We should all strive to make others feel the same way we wish to feel every time we come into contact with a fellow human being. In the workplace in particular, where we spend most of our time, creating a space that is inclusive and where people feel like they belong is key to creating a healthy work environment where every employee can thrive by being connected to, and engaged with, their work and their colleagues.

**Inclusion
is the feeling
of being heard,
seen, and valued
for who we are.**

2

REJECTION AND DEPRECIATION

While this book focuses on inclusion and the inclusive workplace, it is important to discuss rejection and depreciation because these often happen when there is no inclusion. While the focus remains on how to create an inclusive workplace, this cannot be done without discussing what happens when there is a lack of inclusion and belonging in the workplace. We must fully understand the importance of nurturing an inclusive workplace.

What is rejection? Rejection is what we experience when we are being denied something that we put ourselves forward for. We feel rejected when we are being denied something that we want and that we feel we should have. Rejection is the opposite of acceptance. As human beings, there are few things we fear more in life than rejection. It is interesting that fear of success might be one of the few things that we fear nearly as much as rejection.

This fear of rejection goes back to when we are born.

We want love and connection with our mother. From the time we are born, we instinctively seek to be loved and accepted, initially by our mother and then by every human being we come in contact with throughout life. Deep down in all of us, there is a universal, fundamental desire to be accepted, seen, and loved by other human beings. Rejection is one of the worst experiences that can happen to us. The consequences of rejection on our emotional, mental, spiritual, and physical well-being are profound. Acts of rejection should never be ignored nor the effects of rejection be disregarded. Although as individuals we can control how we react to rejection, we should also acknowledge the deep, devastating impact it causes within ourselves and within others.

What is depreciation? Depreciation is the opposite of appreciation. Depreciation is when someone makes us feel less than we are. Depreciation is anytime someone belittles us, intentionally or unintentionally, making us feel inferior. It happens when there is no inclusion or belonging. Depreciation can be direct or indirect. One frequent indirect way depreciation is delivered is through so-called humor or jokes that are actually a way to make someone feel less than they are. Depreciating jokes should be taken very seriously, especially in the workplace, because their impact on the work environment can be profound and yet also often hard to be pinpointed. The consequences of depreciation on the receiving individual can be devastating and should not be diminished or ignored.

Rejection and depreciation often go together and are

extremely harmful and toxic. When someone is consistently rejected and unappreciated in the workplace, the negative impact on their personal, emotional, spiritual, mental, and physical well-being is significant while the work environment is negatively impacted even beyond that one individual.

During my career in corporations, I observed how certain groups of people tend to emerge as the popular ones, sharing coffee breaks and lunches together and failing to invite others to their team outings. When repeated over and over again, those who are not invited to the party start feeling rejected altogether, and it becomes difficult for them to feel accepted and valued.

When this happens, working together becomes difficult because for the person who has been repeatedly left out, it is hard for them to feel that they work in a safe environment where everyone is valued and respected. Ultimately, they may decide to retreat into silence. I remember attending team meetings where the "cool kids" of the group were always the loudest contributors, and those who were repeatedly left out from team lunches were the silent ones. Ultimately, the team meetings reflected only the voices of the loudest, most outspoken characters, those who had created a group of their own, and the people who were never invited to any social activities were simply never heard.

Business leaders should pay specific attention to even small acts of rejection, depreciative humor, and acts of belittling in the workplace. While they can be hard to notice at first, but particularly as they build up, they are deadly for the organization.

One of my lowest moments as an employee was with a manager who always made me feel rejected and belittled. During our rare, often cancelled or cut-short one-to-ones, my manager would never make eye contact and would spend the entire time typing on her laptop. She would start our one-to-ones by talking about projects she was working on, updates from the leadership team, and other scattered facts and figures.

Whenever she paused for more than a few seconds, I would try to talk about my current projects. Whenever I asked for recommendations or feedback, I would get a vague answer. Even worse, during our team meetings with about 15 colleagues on the conference call, she would ridicule me in front of the entire team. For example, when I shared an update on my team and projects and I suggested a new idea, she would interrupt me, dismiss my idea as "ridiculous" or say "it will never happen," have a good laugh in front of all the other team members, and move on with her agenda. This illustrates exactly what depreciation and rejection look like in the workplace and points to what should be avoided at all costs when creating an inclusive workplace.

Business leaders should
pay specific attention
to even small acts
of rejection,
depreciative humor, and
acts of belittling in
the workplace.
They can be hard to notice
at first, but particularly
as they build up,
they are deadly for the
organization.

3

THE INCLUSIVE WORKPLACE

What is an inclusive workplace? Every time I coach leaders on how to create a diverse and inclusive workplace, I hear the same question: what does an inclusive workplace look like? The truth is that no two workplaces will look the same; however, inclusive workplaces share some common similarities.

Inclusive workplaces have inclusive leaders. Leaders, managers, and team leaders in an inclusive workplace are completely committed to being inclusive leaders. They smile often and sincerely; they make strong eye contact with all employees; they say each employee's name when they address them; and they ask each of them how they are, every day. Inclusive leaders are available to all employees when needed because they know that employees are everything. Inclusive leaders are approachable, humble, and easy to talk to. Inclusive leaders are positive, inspiring, and make everyone feel welcome and valued. Inclusive leaders make each employee feel like they truly matter.

Inclusive leaders lift up the atmosphere in every meeting, every interaction. Inclusive leaders are thoughtful, and they say thank you often. Inclusive leaders acknowledge team member contributions often and reward when appropriate. Inclusive leaders treat everyone the same and show no favoritism to any employee or colleague. Inclusive leaders are fair to everyone.

An inclusive workplace delivers above-average performance in all departments. Inclusive teams have a deep sense of appreciation for each other and collaborate in an efficient manner, leading to above-average results. Sales teams that are inclusive will produce better sales results, marketing teams that are inclusive will produce more effective marketing campaigns, operations teams that are inclusive will produce more effective operations, and so on. This is true with public organizations and with non-profit organizations as well. The idea is teams that nurture a deep sense of appreciation for each other are better positioned to collaborate effectively than teams that do not nurture a sense of appreciation for each other. The difference in the team work outcomes can be significant when there is a deep sense of appreciation compared to outcomes of teams having no sense of appreciation or inclusion.

During my time working for a software company, I was working in the UK office operating as the European Headquarters. At the time, the company operated different business units in North America, the UK and Europe, and in Asia Pacific. The North American business units were divided between the West, the East, and Central. There were additional business units within each geographic area, including Enterprise, Mid-Market, and Small and Medium Businesses. In total, there were about 20 different business units across the world, each operating relatively independently and with their own sales targets and revenue targets.

The UK office was relatively new and had been created almost at the same time as the Asia Pacific office in Sydney. The North American business units were the oldest of the organization's business units and had been operating for several years. Shortly after the UK business unit had been created, I was hired to run the marketing department, working hand in hand with the vice president of the UK office. We rapidly became effective partners, working in an environment of trust, appreciation, communication, and collaboration. From the very first day I joined, the vice president of the UK office made me feel valued, appreciated, and an equal. He built that trust and gave support through active listening, intentional communications, and trusting me to come up with my own ideas and strategies.

Eventually, as months passed and as our team became bigger, we started looking at business performance. It became obvious that our business unit was always in the top three performing business units across the entire organization. Our business unit consistently delivered against our business goals month after month and quarter after quarter. This comparative level of performance happened though other business units were more established, had a wider customer base, were in a more mature market, and had in-house sales operations, inside sales, IT support, and HR support that we did not have. Despite all the odds, we consistently were among the top performing units.

To this day, I am convinced that the reason our business unit was so successful was because of the leadership of an inclusive leader who, in turn, created a highly inclusive workplace where every employee felt valued, appreciated, and like they belonged. In parallel, business units that delivered worse business results were known for having difficult leaders who created tensions and division among different departments. Those under-performing business units had created an excuse culture, where poor performance was blamed on circumstances such as not having the right resources, lacking a sufficient budget, facing a difficult economic context, or operating in a new market. I have observed this correlation between inclusive workplaces and excellent business performance with every single organization I have worked with for the last twelve years across different countries and even with different departments.

Inclusive teams have excellent employee retention rates and employee engagement scores. In an inclusive team, each team member feels valued, respected, heard, and seen, which makes them want to bring their best selves to work every day and also creates a deep connection with their work. Team members in an inclusive team feel strongly engaged and connected with their work and with their colleagues, making them satisfied and happy in their work. This results in higher employee engagement scores and also significantly reduces employee turnover.

When Tim Cook became Apple's CEO in 2011, everyone wondered how Cook could match Steve Jobs' performance. As a passionate believer in diversity and inclusion, Tim Cook appointed three women to the executive team, recruited directors from underrepresented groups, and launched an annual diversity and inclusion report. Since 2014, the percentage of new hires at Apple who are female increased from 31 percent to 36 percent, and the number of females among the under-30 age groups increased from 31 percent to 38 percent. Apple is now considered at the top of the list for diversity and inclusion within the tech sector. Apple's financial performance under Tim Cook has been outstanding. In 2018, Apple earned $265.6 billion, the highest annual revenue in the company's history.[1] Apple has demonstrated that a thoughtful, genuine, and sustained commitment to diversity and inclusion delivers great performances.

Chapter 3 Notes

1. https://www.statista.com/statistics/265125/
   total-net-sales-of-apple-since-2004/

**Inclusive
workplaces
have
inclusive leaders.**

4

WORKPLACE INCLUSION
AND PERFORMANCE

The 2020 Global Startup Outlook from Silicon Valley Bank[1] reported that only a quarter of new businesses (26 percent) are actively trying to increase diversity and inclusion within their leadership teams. It asked new businesses in Canada, the United States, and the United Kingdom about diversity initiatives and less than half (43 percent) said they had company-wide promotion and hiring goals, while fewer than one-in-five had these goals for executive positions (the C-suite). These findings confirm previous research in 2018 from First Round, stating that 78 percent of new business founders have no formal plans or policies in place to promote diversity and inclusion.[2] These recent findings confirm that most businesses are not investing in diversity and inclusion, perhaps simply because they do not understand the business benefit of building highly diverse and inclusive teams. Few businesses are making diversity and inclusion a priority and part of the strategy.

A Boston Consulting Group research report[3] revealed that over a quarter of employees at large companies do not feel that their direct manager is committed to diversity and inclusion. Many line managers have never received any training nor do they have any awareness of diversity and inclusion, despite representing the wider group of role models for employees and having significant power to implement, or ignore, diversity.

Employees whose line managers are not committed to diversity and inclusion are twice as likely to feel excluded at work and are nearly three times more likely to seek employment elsewhere, according to Boston Consulting Group.[4]

Meanwhile, an increasing body of research consistently demonstrates that diverse and inclusive teams are more productive, generate more profits, and create more value. In 2018, McKinsey ran an analysis by drawing on a data set of more than 1,000 companies covering 12 countries.[5] In that research, McKinsey found that companies with better gender diversity are 21 percent more likely to show financial returns above their respective national industry medians and 27 percent more likely to have superior value creation.

Further, firms with better ethnic diversity were 33 percent more likely to financially outperform their respective industry medians. On the other hand, companies in the fourth quartile on both gender and ethnic diversity are 29 percent more likely to underperform their industry peers on profitability. This same McKinsey research also found that gender, ethnic, and cultural diversity, particularly within executive teams, is correlated to financial performance across multiple countries worldwide.

Chapter 4 Notes

1. https://www.svb.com/globalassets/library/uploadedfiles/content/trends_and_insights/reports/startup_outlook_report/suo_global_report_2020-final.pdf

2. https://www.wired.com/story/startup-founders-think-real-progress-diversity-years-away/

3. https://www.bcg.com/publications/2019/fixing-the-flawed-approach-to-diversity

4. https://www.bcg.com/publications/2020/frontline-leaders-make-break-progress-diversity

5. https://www.mckinsey.com/~/media/mckinsey/business%20functions/organization/our%20insights/delivering%20through%20diversity/delivering-through-diversity_full-report.ashx

Employees whose
line managers are not
committed to diversity
and inclusion are twice as
likely to feel excluded
at work and are nearly
three times more likely to
seek employment
elsewhere.

5

HOW DIVERSITY AND INCLUSION DRIVE GROWTH

Diversity and inclusion boost engagement and productivity. Organizations that actively hire diverse talents have higher team collaboration and higher team commitment than non-diverse and non-inclusive ones. CEB, now part of Gartner,[1] found workers in highly diverse and inclusive organizations result in a 26 percent increase in team collaboration and an 18 percent increase in team commitment. Additionally, employees who are part of organizations with high levels of diversity report a 7 percent higher intent to stay than their peers in organizations that have low levels of diversity. Higher employee engagement helps organizations maintain productivity and stand out from competition. Higher employee engagement means that teams go beyond expectations and that makes a significant difference at the organization level.

Diversity and inclusion improve employee satisfaction

and retention. The 2018 ADP report found that employees who trusted their team leader were 12 times more likely to be fully engaged,[2] and 51 percent of workers say that they feel belonging in the workplace when they can freely share their opinions, while 50 percent say they feel like they belong when they feel comfortable being fully themselves,[3] to which end being part of a diverse and inclusive team makes a big difference. In fact, ADP found that teamwork was the biggest driver of engagement, and employees who identified as part of a team were 2.3 times more likely to be fully engaged.

Diversity and inclusion enhance organizational success through a collaborative culture. A Harvard Business Review article reported that inclusiveness isn't just nice to have on teams. Further research shows that it directly enhances performance. Teams with inclusive leaders are 17 percent more likely to report that they are high performing, 20 percent more likely to say they make high-quality decisions, and 29 percent more likely to report behaving collaboratively. What's more, there was a 10 percent improvement in perceptions that inclusion increases work attendance by almost one day a year per employee, reducing the cost of absenteeism.[4]

Diversity and inclusion help organizations win over top talent. A Glassdoor survey revealed that two-thirds (67 percent) of jobseekers say a diverse workforce is an important factor when evaluating companies and job offers. The Glassdoor survey also found that when it comes to the recruiting process, minority groups value diversity even more than the average job seeker. Seventy-two percent of women surveyed say that a diverse workforce is important when evaluating companies and job offers, along with 89 percent of black respondents, 80 percent of Asians, and 70 percent of Latinx.

Military veterans also care about workforce diversity with 65 percent reporting that they consider it an important factor during the job search process. Interestingly, the survey also revealed that when it comes to leadership diversity, two in five people (41 percent) do not think their company has a diverse executive team. The over-whelming majority (89 percent) said that their company's executive team was male, and more than three-fourths (78 percent) also indicated that their executive teams include white executives.[5]

Organizations that want to attract top talent must transform the way they think and act about diversity and inclusion in order to be successful. Diversity and inclusion significantly improve cultural appreciation and lower risks of discrimination. Businesses that actively hire diverse talents create opportunities for employees to spend more time with individuals from different backgrounds, which increases their appreciation for different cultures and ways of thinking and reduces negative thoughts like racism and sexism. In the context of Black Lives Matter and #MeToo, businesses will particularly benefit from mitigating racism and sexism in the workplace by hiring diverse talents because the risks of employee lawsuits, bad publicity, and brand damage due to racism and sexism are at an all-time high. Many tech investors now include #MeToo clauses[6] in startup deals to prevent sexism, and more new businesses now include anti-racism in their diversity and inclusion pledge like UK travel expert Pluto's plan.[7]

Diversity and inclusion significantly increase innovation. Diverse management teams are more innovative than less diverse teams, confirmed Boston Consulting Group[8] after surveying 1700 companies. Companies with above-average diversity produce a greater proportion of revenue from innovation (45 percent of total) than companies with below average diversity (26 percent). Members of diverse companies see things in a variety of ways. They recognize new market opportunities, and they can better identify unmet market needs. This is especially critical in current COVID-19 times where new consumer needs are rapidly emerging. Businesses that actively hire diverse teams innovate faster and better than their competitors and will emerge from the COVID pandemic stronger.

Diversity and inclusion create more agility which is critical for business recovery. The ability to spot and seize game changers in a crisis like COVID-19 is likely to be mission-critical, as reported by McKinsey. Strategic agility is stronger in companies that can draw on the full spectrum of diverse talent. According to McKinsey, "Our research and the research of others suggest that when companies invest in diversity and inclusion, they are in a better position to create more adaptive, effective teams and are more likely to recognize diversity as a competitive advantage. Meanwhile, other companies might struggle."[9] Businesses that prioritize hiring diverse talents will benefit from strategic agility, which will position them for success during and after COVID.

Diversity and inclusion significantly increase sound decision-making. Recent research found that racially homogeneous teams are less rigorous in their decision-making and make more mistakes than diverse ones. "One project demonstrated that when you tell students that they're going to be having a discussion regarding a written article, they prepare more rigorously if they know that they're going to have to debate in a more diverse group," said Evan Apfelbaum, Career Development Professor of Management at the MIT Sloan School.[10]

Businesses hiring diverse talents increase their chances of sound and better decision-making, which will position them for success in a COVID world or other times of adversity or disruption. "Diversity winners that deploy a systematic approach to inclusion and diversity and don't fear bold action to foster inclusion and belonging are most likely to reap the rewards. Now is the time to be even bolder," reported McKinsey[11] in its May 2020 report "Diversity still matters."

Diversity and inclusion significantly help market to a broader consumer group. Diversity broadens your customer base. By having a diverse workforce, you are more likely to learn about the concerns and preferences of various population segments. This allows you to adjust your products or services to make them more enticing to these groups, potentially leading to an increase in your number of customers. A business with a diverse group of individuals, all of whom feel supported and included, enables more effective marketing to a broader consumer group and taps into related business opportunities. This can be a matter of survival for many early-stage businesses.

With cultural diversity come different languages and even different ways to speak the same language. English is a global language, and a big part of the global workforce speaks it natively or to a high level. Covering many languages will come in handy with actions directed toward a specific target and/or country, and there will be no chance for the message to get lost in translation. Languages like Spanish, Portuguese, and French are spoken in many countries globally in very similar but also very different ways. Having people who speak the same language but who are from different parts of the world is an excellent competitive advantage.

When I led the European marketing department of an American software company, all marketing campaigns were initially created from the North American headquarters. As I got to meet with some of our European customers, I quickly realized that they wanted something different, and in particular, they wanted a more European approach. We started listening to what our

European customers wanted, we came up with a plan, and we tested it. One request in particular was to have local events in the local language where they could meet with their peers in the local ecosystem. For the first time in the history of the company, we hosted local events in French for our French customers because we listened to suggestions from our French employees about how to approach the local market. The response was overwhelmingly positive: hundreds of French customers, prospects, and partners registered for our event. The audience was highly engaged during the event with many questions, comments, and much interaction. The brand awareness hit an all-time high, especially on social media, and we even created new revenue and pipeline at the back of the event. All of this was equivalent to more than five times the investment in the event. By leveraging our French team and listening to their insights into how to best approach their market, we created a new form of marketing that generated one of the most successful marketing campaigns in our business unit.

Diversity and inclusion significantly enhance brand reputation, which is good for sales. If your company isn't viewed as being inclusive, some customers (including both in the B2B and B2C marketplaces) may shy away from giving you their business. This is especially true with Millennial and Gen Z customers. These two generations are incredibly socially conscious. As a result, they may prefer inclusive companies when considering purchases in both their personal and professional lives. If you aren't seen as supporting diversity, you may miss out on opportunities to increase sales, foster strong customer relationships, and, ultimately, enhance your profitability.

Chapter 5 Notes

1. https://www.icmi.com/resources/2018/what-diversity-and-inclusion-mean-for-employee-engagement#:~:text=It%20also%20found%20that%20engaged,18%25%20increase%20in%20team%20commitment.

2. https://www.adp.com/-/media/adp/ResourceHub/pdf/ADPRI/ADPRI0102_2018_Engagement_Study_Technical_Report_RELEASE%20READY.ashx

3. Ibid.

4. https://hbr.org/2019/03/why-inclusive-leaders-are-good-for-organizations-and-how-to-become-one#:~:text=Inclusiveness%20isn't%20just%20nice,likely%20to%20report%20behaving%20collaboratively.

5. https://www.glassdoor.com/about-us/twothirds-people-diversity-important-deciding-work-glassdoor-survey-2/

6. https://www.ft.com/content/5d4ef400-4732-11e9-b168-96a37d002cd3

7. https://www.phocuswire.com/pluto-travel-startup-pledge-for-antiracism-diversity-and-inclusion

8. https://www.bcg.com/publications/2018/how-diverse-leadership-teams-boost-innovation

9. https://www.mckinsey.com/featured-insights/diversity-and-inclusion/diversity-still-matters

10. https://sloanreview.mit.edu/article/the-trouble-with-homogeneous-teams/

11. https://www.mckinsey.com/featured-insights/diversity-and-inclusion/diversity-still-matters

If your company
isn't viewed as being
inclusive,
some customers may
shy away from
giving you
their business.

6

HOW STARTUP MYTHS ON DIVERSITY HOLD BACK INNOVATION

We live in a world that is increasingly relying on technology in every facet of our lives. In every industry, organizations are increasingly adopting new technology to satisfy the demand of today's customers. As a result, new technologies and new startups are becoming more prevalent and are having a bigger impact on how companies operate with these new technologies. However, popular myths on startups and their lack of diversity and inclusion are significantly holding innovation back. Let's take a deeper look.

The first images that appear when searching "startup founder" in Google are those of young and middle-aged white men. The first books that appear when searching "startup founder books" are written by young and middle-aged white men: Eric Ries *The Lean Startup*, Ben Horowitz *The Hard Thing About Hard Things*, Peter Thiel *Zero to One* to name three.

BBC news[1] reported the story of Gymshark's worth over £1bn, opening the article with "Ben Francis started Gymshark from his parents' garage in 2012 when he was 19 years old." The first images that appear when searching "startup events" on Google are those of young and middle-aged white men again. Listed at the top of the most inspiring movies for entrepreneurs comes *The Social Network*, a movie about how a young white man, Mark Zuckerberg, founded his startup Facebook at 19 years old out of his college dorm room at Harvard University.

The representation of startup founders is consistent in every image, book, media, or event: a young or middle-aged white man. This vast amount of media consumption shapes how we see the world we live in. Images can shape our views of reality. Studies show that audiences substitute stereotypes they see on screen for reality when they have not had any direct interactions with particular groups.

A *Forbes* article reports, "In addition to aggravating racial tensions, the erasure and negative portrayals of people of color can adversely affect how people of color see themselves. Prolonged television exposure predicts a decrease in self-esteem for all girls and for black boys, and an increase in self-esteem for white boys. These differences correlate with the racial and gender biases in Hollywood, which casts only white men as heroes, while erasing or subordinating other groups as villains, sidekicks, and sexual objects."[2]

It is no wonder then that the myth of the young or middle aged white male startup founder becomes a self-perpetuating prophecy and that any other group of people is largely under-represented. According to the EEOC, 83% of tech executives are white.[3] A Gender Gap Grader study shows that women represent 9% of developers in the startup ecosystem and 4.2% of software architects.[4] A 2020 article from the Next Web wrote, "Almost half of Indian startups don't hire women, to save on maternity costs."[5] It is not only the founders who are white male but even startup workforce is male and usually white.

So why should startup founders care about attracting and retaining a diverse workforce? Why should investors fund diverse startups and even encourage startup founders to diversify their workforce? The significant benefits of building a diverse startup team are increased creativity, faster problem-solving, and greater diversity of thought that opens up new market opportunities and creates more revenue streams. The list goes on: better understanding of the customer base can lead to building better products as a result and thereby, increasing revenue and customer retention. Diversity in the workplace also leads to increased employee engagement and productivity and that leads to keeping a competitive edge. Presented below are six startup myths on diversity and inclusion that hold innovation back and that you should be aware of.

Myth #1: Startup founders are young. As mentioned earlier, the myth of the young startup founder who built his app in his parents' garage is everywhere. Google, Apple, Microsoft, Amazon, Disney, HP, and Facebook—the media can't get enough of the legend of the young entrepreneur starting in the parental garage. Although it's a fascinating myth, a 2019 influential academic study by the Kellogg School of Management, Northwestern University[6] shows just how misguided the popular narrative is. Economists Pierre Azoulay, Benjamin Jones, Daniel Kim, and Javier Miranda analyzed administrative government data on the founders of all US businesses that were started during the eight-year period of 2007 to 2014. The authors calculated the average founder age (at the time of founding) along with key startup characteristics (industry, financing, patenting, location) and outcomes (hyper-growth, acquisition, or IPO). According to this study, here is the average founder age along each of these dimensions:

- All companies (with at least one employee): average age 42

- Fastest growing 0.1% of companies: average age 45

- High-tech industry: average age 43

- Venture-backed: average age 42

- Filed patents: average age 45

- Successfully exited (acquisition or IPO): average age 47

- Located in Silicon Valley: average age 42

- Located in an entrepreneurial hub: average age 41

According to this academic research, founders in their twenties and thirties are less likely to start high-growth companies compared with their share of total companies founded. Conversely, founders 40 years old and above are more likely to start high-growth businesses relative to their contribution of total companies founded. The average age of startup founders is more or less around 40 years of age—far greater than the popular narrative of the mid-20s college dropout. Finally, the study shows that conditional on starting a company, the probability of achieving "high-success" (fastest growing 0.1% of firms or successful exit) is lowest for founders in their early twenties and increases in a linear fashion along with founder age up to the late fifties.

Myth #2: Startups founders are men. What is the first name that come to mind when thinking about startup founders? Mark Zuckerberg? Steve Jobs? Bill Gates? According to a 2017 Crunchbase study, only 17% had a female startup founder that year.[7] According to research by All Raise,[8] only 15% of venture capital funding is allocated to female founders. A lot of this gender imbalance is due to unconscious bias at the funding stage. One 2018 study[9] in the *Academy of Management Journal* found that, during investment pitches, female entrepreneurs are more likely to be asked "prevention" questions—questions related to safety and potential risks and losses. In contrast, male entrepreneurs are more likely to be asked "promotion" questions—questions related to their hopes, ambitions, and achievements.

However, the business case for female funded startups is clear: A Boston Consulting Group study[10] revealed that, for every dollar of investment raised, female-run start-ups generated 78 cents in revenue, whereas male-run startups generated only 31 cents. Women outperformed their male counterparts despite raising less money ($935K versus $2.12M). These findings are consistent with several other studies. Data collected by First Round Capital[11] found that the female-founder companies it had funded performed 63% better than the all-male founding teams it had funded. Additionally, research from the Ewing Marion Kauffman Foundation[12] found that women-led teams generate a 35% higher return on investment than all-male teams. Research clearly shows that women outperformed their male counterparts despite raising less money.

Myth #3: Startup founders don't have children. According to the popular narrative of the young male startup founder in his garage, startup founders don't have kids. This narrative clearly disregards some great examples of successful mom entrepreneurs and startup founders. The Baby Einstein Company was founded in 1997 by stay-at-home mom Julie Aigner-Clark at her home in Georgia. Aigner-Clark and her husband invested $18,000 of their savings to produce the initial product, a Video Board Book, a VHS entitled Baby Einstein, later sold as Language Nursery. They saw the opportunity to develop products that assist in the intellectual development of a child from a very early age. Baby Einstein grew revenues from $1 million in 1998 to over $10 million just a few years later in 2000. This growth, rapid brand recognition, and the quality of the products caught the eye of The Walt Disney Company, who acquired the business for an undisclosed amount in 2001. For about eight years following the acquisition, the value of the brand continued to multiply and was rumored to be valued at $400 million at one point.

Sheila Lirio Marcelo's inspiration to found Care.com was based on solving a problem that she knew was not just her own. A young mother with two small children, Sheila was challenged to find quality child care solutions. She knew there had to be a better way than using the phone book or asking the neighbors if they knew a good sitter. Sheila founded Care.com in 2006 and today, the company is the largest online care destination in the world, with more than 10.7 million members across 16 countries.[13]

Little Mizz[14] was founded by mother of two, Nicole Gleeson. Little Mizz provides a monthly hands-on activity kit based on five specific pillars: Life Lessons, Fitness, Nutrition, How To's, and Arts and Crafts with the goal of inspiring creativity and confidence in girls from an early age. Kits can include everything from lessons in etiquette and fun dance routines to recipes for nutritious snacks and do-it-yourself jewelry making.

The transferable skills from moms to startup founders are many: the ability to be flexible, to prioritize, and to be efficient with limited time are all critical skills for startup founders that should not be underestimated by investors.

Myth #4: Startup founders are white. The current conversation around systematic racism is especially relevant in the startup ecosystem where non-white founders have long been ignored, under-represented, and overlooked. The reality is that non-white startup founders not only exist but are extremely successful and should be highlighted more in the media, in the movies, in books, and in podcasts to share their success stories. Here are some powerful examples of successful black startup founders.

Nana Addison was born in Ghana and raised in Germany. She is a self-titled Afropean and a tech entrepreneur who has founded not one, but two companies. Addison is the brains behind CURL, the creative agency behind CURL CON, Germany's hair, beauty, and culture convention which caters to the textures and darker skin tones in the DACH beauty world. She also launched Stylindi, a booking and product shopping platform for the independent hair and beauty community, in 2017.[15]

Gerald Manu's entrepreneurial tendencies started from an early age; he famously built his fashion business Devacci through selling crisps and drinks at school in Croydon, London, generating little more than £10 per day. Forward a few years and Devacci is a fully-fledged wearable tech brand, selling thousands of his designs per month, with a team of five employees. You can find Devacci in a dedicated online store, and more recently, in the aisles of TJ Maxx, who offered to stock the line.[16]

Emilia Makosa is a London-based entrepreneur who answered the call of Black women struggling with hyperpigmentation. Her complete cosmeceutical skin-care collection caters exclusively to Black skin. After a struggle with acne, she founded Emeilleurq, a luxury skincare and lifestyle brand with a total of 13 products, ranging from cleansers to toners to spot treatments, and an intensive moisturizer.[17]

Myth #5: Startup founders are straight. The popular narrative of the white male startup founder comes with the assumption that he is also straight. Mark Zuckerberg is well-known for the Chan Zuckerberg Initiative founded with his wife Priscilla Chan. Bill and Melinda Gates are equally well-known for their foundation, the Bill and Melinda Gates Foundation. However, LGBTQ+ people have had an immense impact on the tech industry, from founders to venture capitalists to innovators. Here are some success stories of LGBTQ+ startup trail blazers.

Joel Simkhai is the cofounder of Grindr, a social networking app for gay, bisexual, trans, and queer people. The company, which was a subsidiary of Beijing Kunlun Tech, was acquired in March 2020 by San Vicente Acquisition for $620 million.[18]

Arlan Hamilton is the founder and managing partner

at Backstage Capital, a VC firm that invests in women, people of color, and LGBT founders.[19]

Myth #6 Startup founders are atheists or Christian. It is a well-recognized fact that Venture Capitalists, typically eager to back apps with the potential to reach billions of users, are more standoffish when it comes to startups with Muslim founders or ones that are targeted for a Muslim audience. Mashable[20] recently wrote that "ignorance and fear are big obstacles for Muslim startup founders." However, Muslim startup founders represent a unique opportunity for investors to reach the 2 billion Muslim people in the world. Here are a few successful examples of Muslim startup founders.

When Rashid Dar moved to New York City to complete graduate school, the Muslim entrepreneur found it challenging to locate quiet spaces to perform Salah, his five daily obligatory prayers. "I'd find myself praying in dressing rooms at H&M, in empty stairwells, or on the side of a highway," Dar said. These experiences led him to start Musallah in 2015, a mobile app that crowdsources prayer locations across the globe. Dar's app, which has the chance to be used by more than one billion Muslims worldwide, hasn't been met with millions in venture cash. He turned to Kickstarter, where it drew more than $14,000 in backing.[21]

Navid Akhtar is the Founder and CEO of Alchemiya, a global streaming and Video-On-Demand (VOD) platform that showcases the best films docs and lifestyle content from across the Muslim world. Launched in 2015, he has contributed to its successful growth, with paying customers in over 40 countries, and recent inclusion as an 'add on' channel on Amazon Prime.[22]

Shabed, co-founder of Affinis Labs,[23] an incubator for business with a positive impact on Muslim communities, says, "I believe that entrepreneurship is a good deterrent to prejudice and racism. If you can enhance someone's life through a product, they're going to look at you differently." He added, "And now is not the time to abandon your Muslim customers, either. The Muslim customers are doubling down on their identity."

Startup founders can be older, female, moms, non-white, LGBT+, and non-Christian, and they can be even more successful than many young, straight, white men startup founders as we demonstrated earlier. These underrepresented startup founders often bring more innovation, open up interesting new markets, and represent a unique untapped potential for the global economy and for their potential investors.

On the other hand, startup founders who are young or middle-aged, straight, white men can increase creativity, innovation, problem-solving, diversity of thought, and build better products by actively diversifying their workforce. Startup founders should diversify their workforce as early as possible—even when they are still building their team—because this will give them a unique competitive edge and set them up for success.

From this research it is clear that for better investment opportunities, angel investors, accelerators and incubators, venture capital firms, and corporate investors should diversify startup founder types just as they diversify their assets.

Chapter 6 Notes

1. https://www.bbc.co.uk/news/business-53781515

2. https://www.forbes.com/sites/quora/2019/05/22/
   why-is-equal-representation-in-media-
   important/?sh=65b42d652a84

3. https://www.techrepublic.com/
   article/5-eye-opening-statistics-about-minorities-in-tech/

4. https://www.virginstartup.org/how-to/
   how-address-startup-gender-gap

5. https://thenextweb.com/growth-quarters/2020/03/09/
   almost-half-of-indian-startups-dont-hire-women-to-save-
   on-maternity-costs/

6. https://www.kellogg.northwestern.edu/faculty/
   jones-ben/htm/Age%20and%20High%20Growth%20
   Entrepreneurship.pdf

7. https://news.crunchbase.com/news/
   q1-2019-diversity-report-female-founders-own-17-
   percent-of-venture-dollars/

8. https://www.allraise.org/

9. https://journals.aom.org/doi/abs/10.5465/amj.2016.1215

10. https://www.bcg.com/en-us/publications/2018/
    why-women-owned-startups-are-better-bet

11. http://10years.firstround.com/

12. https://www.kauffmanfellows.org/wp-content/uploads/
    KFR_Vol7/Juliana_Garaizar_vol7.pdf

13. https://www.annualreports.com/HostedData/
    AnnualReports/PDF/NYSE_CRCM_2018.pdf

50 • INCLUSION

14. https://www.forbes.com/sites/brentgleeson/2014/06/12/3-great-examples-of-successful-mom-entrepreneurs/

15. https://www.eu-startups.com/2020/07/10-black-startup-founders-in-europe-to-watch-in-2020-and-beyond/

16. Ibid.

17. https://www.eu-startups.com/2020/07/10-black-startup-founders-in-europe-to-watch-in-2020-and-beyond/

18. https://pitchbook.com/blog/lgbtq-founders-entrepreneurs-and-vcs-you-should-know

19. Ibid.

20. https://mashable.com/2016/05/22/muslim-entrepreneurs/?europe=true

21. Ibid.

22. Ibid.

23. Ibid.

Female entrepreneurs
are more likely
to be asked
"prevention" questions
by investors.
In contrast,
male entrepreneurs
are more likely
to be asked
"promotion" questions.

7

CREATING AND NURTURING YOUR INCLUSIVE WORKPLACE

Embed diversity and inclusion in your mission statement. The first place to start with diversity and inclusion for your organization is to start with the why. Ask yourself why diversity and inclusion are important to your organization. How will diversity and inclusion in your company help grow and scale your business? What is it about diversity and inclusion that will fundamentally drive all the things you will do with your business?

Is it because you believe that having a diverse and inclusive workforce will help you better understand your consumers who are also diverse and, therefore, build better products that your customers will love? Is it because you think that diverse and inclusive teams work better together and are faster at problem solving and will execute better and, therefore, you will have a competitive advantage? Is it because having a diverse and inclusive workforce will force your business to think differently, to build more innovative apps and products, and to generate more revenue through innovation? Whatever the reason is for what makes diversity and inclusion an important value for your organization, you must take the time to craft your answer, clearly articulate why this is important, and write it down.

Set goals and implement a framework. Only a quarter of start-ups (26 percent) are actively trying to increase diversity within their leadership teams, according to Silicon Valley Bank.[1] Less than half (43 percent) of companies have company-wide promotion and hiring goals for diversity, while fewer than one-in-five have these goals for executive positions (the C-suite). Roughly 78 percent of new business founders[2] have no formal plans or policies in place to promote diversity and inclusion. We could speculate about why that is and consider whether perhaps it is because they expect someone else to take ownership.

The point is that nothing will happen unless you set goals, or rather, nothing will happen unless you set goals tied to monetary compensation. Goals drive behavior. Monetary goals drive behavior faster. If you are committed to diversity and inclusion, you must set goals for your leadership team that are tied to monetary bonuses. I recommend 30 percent of the bonus be directly linked to the diversity and inclusion goals. Having worked with numerous tech organizations and having had countless conversations on diversity and inclusion, I have witnessed that setting diversity goals that are financially rewarded is the only route to success.

Inclusive organizations are **twice** more likely to exceed financial targets (Deloitte Research).[3] And 85 percent of CEOs whose companies have an inclusiveness strategy report that it's improved their bottom line according to a PWC CEO Survey.[4] For companies ranking in the top quartile of executive board diversity, return on equity (ROE) was 53 percent higher as reported in a McKinsey Diversity Study,[5] while companies with the most women board directors outperformed those with the least number of women on invested capital return (ROIC) by 26 percent reported in Catalyst's 2011 study.[6] There are many, many more studies available that demonstrate the return of investment on diversity and inclusion, so investing in a budget to reward diversity and inclusion will pay back.

More organizations are understanding that investing in diversity is key to business recovery. In October 2020, British rail leader Northern Railway[7] was creating more than 160 new roles to encourage the next generation of Black, ethnic minority, female, and younger employees to join its workforce. Demonstrating its commitment to diversity and inclusion, the operator runs a range of employee inclusion groups, boasts a 250-strong employee engagement group, and runs an extensive equality, diversity, and inclusion events calendar. This initiative to increase diversity is part of a wider campaign by the UK rail industry called "Powering rail productivity: The case for greater diversity."[8]

Build your inclusive team. Once you have done the

basics—understanding why diversity and inclusion are important to your business, incorporating diversity and inclusion in your mission statement, and setting diversity goals tied to monetary outcomes—you must set up a process to constantly monitor, adjust, and improve your diversity and inclusion practices. Imagine implementing a new program and having the policy in place and simply expecting it to work organically. It would be naive to expect success from a diversity and inclusion (D&I) initiative without investing more resources to monitor, assess, adjust, and improve it.

This is why I encourage you to appoint a diversity and inclusion taskforce whose mission is to monitor progress, evaluate results, and improve the diversity and inclusion initiatives. Your D&I taskforce must be sponsored by an executive in order to be successful. Having an executive leader on this taskforce will give it the budget, authority, and access to resources it needs to make an impact. You can choose how many people will be part of the taskforce, who will be involved, and how often they will meet. What's important here is that you set up a taskforce that's sponsored by an executive and that it has clear, defined goals. The D&I taskforce goals should be aligned with your new mission statement and with the diversity and inclusion goals that you previously set. I recommend asking your team who is interested in joining the taskforce and making it a voluntary role rather than a mandatory one. People who volunteer are more likely to feel personally committed to the success of the taskforce, regardless of their role in your organization.

Assess your own diversity and inclusion. At this point, as you get started with your organization's D&I programs, a good place to start is determining your current workforce diversity and inclusion. You should start by measuring how diverse and inclusive your workforce is today so that you can track progress as you start your own D&I journey. Here are some components you should look at:

- Make a list of your organization's last ten promotions: How diverse do you consider them in terms of gender, ethnicity, and background?

- Make a list of your organization's last ten hires: How diverse do you consider them in terms of gender, ethnicity, and background?

- If you haven't made enough recent promotions or hires to know, think about your last several all-hands meetings and whose efforts you've acknowledged. Think about the last raises and bonuses you've allocated. Are you distributing rewards and recognition in a way that acknowledges a wide-ranging set of contributions?

- Think about the last five people to leave your organization. Do you notice any commonality in their circumstances or background?

If you see patterns emerging, this gives you a better sense of your starting point and potential areas to prioritize.

I also recommend running a survey measuring employee

engagement to give you a sense of how included your employees feel. You might ask them to answer anonymously the following questions:

- I'm proud to work for [insert company name]. (1 to 10)

- I would recommend [insert company name] as a great place to work. (1 to 10)

- I rarely think about looking for a job at another company. (1 to 10)

- I see myself still working at [insert company name] in two years' time. (1 to 10)

- [insert company name] motivates me to go beyond what I would in a similar role elsewhere. (1 to 10)

Finally, I recommend not only looking at your current workforce composition in terms of gender, race, ethnic background, disability, LGBT+, and age but looking at your leadership workforce composition as well. You might see different numbers. Compare your results with the population of the city/country you live in. If you live in the UK where the non-white population is about 20 percent, you should have about 20 percent non-white in your organization. In London, about 40 percent of the population is non-white, so you should have about 40 percent of your organization workforce being non-white if all your employees are in London. This should give you a benchmark to start with.

According to the United States Census Bureau, based on the 2019 survey, 76.3 percent of the US population is classified as white alone.[9] Organizations in the United States may use this figure as a benchmark to compare their own workforce diversity. Of course, the percentage may vary in specific geographic regions and each geographic region should look at their specific statistics. It is a good exercise to research your local population diversity statistics and use them as a benchmark to assess your own organization's workforce diversity.

Become a change agent. Accountability starts with you. As a business leader, you must create a diversity and inclusion framework that creates a culture of inclusion, and you need to personally buy into it and commit to it. Your support, commitment, and accountability are essential elements for the implementation of a systematic process of inclusion at the workplace. In other words, you should not say things like "We have a candidate pipeline problem." or "There are not enough diverse candidates out there." or "We need to focus on revenue right now." or even "We are too busy right now. We don't have time to focus on diversity and inclusion at the moment."

These types of statements are exactly the opposite of what diversity and inclusion accountability is and why D&I efforts fail. Instead, you can say things like "We will find diverse candidates whatever it takes." or "We will always prioritize diversity and inclusion even in a challenging economic environment, because we know it will help our organization succeed."

Accountability starts with you. You need to feel personally responsible for the success of diversity and inclusion in your organization—without expecting someone else to do this for you—whether you are the CEO, the head of marketing, or the head of HR. Whatever made you read this guide is probably the same reason you feel personally committed to bringing diversity and inclusion in your organization. You are the change agent. Be accountable. Don't make excuses. Take responsibility to educate yourself on this topic, seek expert advice, hold your leadership accountable every day.

Starbucks made the decision to link executive pay to efforts to increase diversity at the company with a target of employing 30 percent Black, indigenous, and people of color employees at the corporate level and 40 percent in retail and manufacturing by 2025.[10] The leading coffee chain has long understood how diversity is key to productivity, as they famously closed 8,000 stores to give staff half a day of diversity training in 2018.

Debias your organization. In an interview I gave to Diginomica in August 2020, I explained that unconscious bias training helps create an excellence-driven tech organization *as long as it takes a multi-pronged approach.* There is a lot of controversy about unconscious bias training and its effectiveness. As a diversity consultant in tech and having helped countless organizations with diversity training, here is my advice.

Unconscious bias training works well when it is done

in the right way. First, this training must have the right content. The content should be structured around real life workplace situations versus just presenting science and research. The training should be action-oriented. Unconscious bias training must include the right audience: leadership. Top leadership, including the CEO, should attend the training to fully understand what it is, buy into it, and commit to being held accountable for fighting unconscious bias proactively at the organizational level.

Unconscious bias training is successful when there is the right context. This training must include why it is important and how it ties to real business outcomes and to the business mission. Unless there is clear articulation about how this kind of training ties to a business outcome, it will fail. Startups must evaluate the impact of the training. By measuring employee engagement in strategies mitigating bias before and after the training, the organization ensures that the training impact goes beyond just the week the training is conducted and that outcome is measured and evaluated consistently thereafter.

Just as with any D&I training, I recommend that unconscious bias training be made voluntary and not mandatory. If made mandatory, either of these initiatives could backfire and have a counter-productive impact. I also really recommend that unconscious bias training be repeated over time. I recommend every three months at the very least to remind employees about implicit biases.

Finally, I recommend that you (the diversity champion), strike a balance between limiting defensiveness about unconscious bias yet clearly communicating the importance of managing bias. Defensiveness is a quite common response to unconscious bias training, so it is critical that the training is positioned in a way that limits defensiveness and articulates the benefits.

UK fintech startup Salary Finance has invested in diversity and inclusion training for its senior leadership, HR team, and all hiring managers to remove unconscious bias in hiring and promoting. Salary Finance understood very early on how removing bias at the organizational level would boost productivity. Asesh Sarkar, CEO of Salary Finance, shared his vision for diversity and inclusion with the company shortly after acquiring Neyber and started investing in awareness training for all line managers involved in the hiring and promoting process. In an interview he shared for my YouTube channel in December 2020, Asesh said, "The whole reason we are successful is because there is diversity of thinking, diversity of experiences, diversity of education, and a diversity of backgrounds."

Chapter 7 Notes

1. https://www.svb.com/globalassets/library/uploadedfiles/content/trends_and_insights/reports/startup_outlook_report/suo_global_report_2020-final.pdf

2. https://www.wired.com/story/startup-founders-think-real-progress-diversity-years-away/

3. https://www2.deloitte.com/content/dam/insights/us/articles/4209_Diversity-and-inclusion-revolution/DI_Diversity-and-inclusion-revolution.pdf

4. https://www.pwc.com/gx/en/diversity-inclusion/best-practices/assets/the-pwc-diversity-journey.pdf

5. https://www.mckinsey.com/business-functions/organization/our-insights/is-there-a-payoff-from-top-team-diversity#:~:text=Diversity%20and%20performance,those%20in%20the%20bottom%20quartile.

6. https://www.catalyst.org/research/the-bottom-line-corporate-performance-and-womens-representation-on-boards-2004-2008/

7. https://media.northernrailway.co.uk/news/northern-creates-160-new-rolesand-launches-new-campaign-to-attract-anew-generation-of-people

8. https://www.railstaff.co.uk/2019/09/25/powering-rail-productivity-the-case-for-greater-diversity/

9. https://www.census.gov/quickfacts/fact/table/US/PST045219

10. https://www.cnbc.com/2020/10/14/starbucks-to-have-30percent-of-corporate-staff-identify-as-a-minority-by-2025.html

**Nothing will happen
unless you set goals,
or rather,
nothing will happen
unless you set goals
tied to monetary
compensation.**

8

BECOMING AN INCLUSIVE LEADER IS A JOURNEY

I came to work that morning feeling tearful, enraged, hurt, and angry. I could no longer take the constant daily verbal and non-verbal aggressions from my manager and from the rest of my team. I had reached the limit of what I could possibly take on without breaking down. I had been working at that company for nearly two years. During that time, I had two managers, and my current manager made me feel unappreciated, unimportant, and more like an annoyance to be dealt with than a valued member of the team. Luckily for me, she was based in San Francisco while I was based in London, so we did not see each other every day apart from the conference calls.

I was also lucky to have a mentor in my office who was acting as my manager out of his pure free will and because he knew it was the right thing to do. That morning I think my mentor could see how agitated I was, so he invited me for a coffee so we could chat. As soon as we sat down behind closed doors and he asked me how I was, I could feel the floodgates opening, and I started crying. When I finally managed to compose myself, I explained to him that I felt insulted by my manager on a daily basis and that I had never been treated so badly in my entire life by anyone. I told him about Zoom calls with my manager and how she would never make eye contact, never ask me how I was, and never ask me anything for the matter. She would just talk at me while typing on her laptop and then she would always finish with "I have to go now, bye," leaving me unheard, unseen, and completely unappreciated.

When I finished sharing my story, my mentor paused and told me that he, too, had reached a low point and had handed in his resignation letter to our CEO a few weeks before. I was shocked by the news. He told me that the CEO had gotten back to him and tried everything to keep him. He initially declined the offer but eventually, after many back and forth conversations, he accepted the offer to stay, and they negotiated a better agreement.

The point to this story is not that my mentor had resigned and then decided to stay. The point was that as a leader, he intentionally made himself vulnerable and shared a very personal story with me. I felt he understood what I was experiencing and that he would help me learn how to deal with my difficult situation. He made me feel included as a valuable part of the team.

Inclusive leaders are those leaders who can change a

situation for the better in moments of crisis. Inclusive leaders are the glue that hold teams together. Inclusive leaders are vulnerable, authentic, humble, inspiring, helpful, and rare. Inclusive leadership is not reserved for a few select people, and it is certainly not a skill or trait that people are born with or without. Inclusive leadership is a journey, and traveling on this journey will be a growing and learning experience.

Listen and learn. "How are you?" My mentor Steve always started our one-to-one meetings with these three simple words: "How are you?" He paid attention while I answered, listening with intention, not interrupting. If he sensed a hesitation or if I brought up a concern, he would ask more questions. One particular thing that I always appreciated about Steve is that he would never try to tell me what to do or how to do it or to "get over" something. He would simply ask me more questions, good questions. He would let me come up with my own answers. Steve made me feel not only seen and heard but also valued and respected. He created a space where I could be my authentic self because he paid attention to what I was saying without distractions.

His leadership style was reflected in our team connection. Knowing we had each other's back, each of us felt empowered to make decisions in faith and not in fear of what might happen if the outcome was not the expected one. Each of us treated our team members in the same inclusive way. We would always make time for one-to-ones with our team members, and we would listen more and speak less. When we listened, we listened with the intention of learning. As this approach cascaded down to all members of our team, it created an inclusive team.

Listening is one of two of the most important attributes of an inclusive leader. Simple yet often not implemented, this strategy makes all the difference between a successful team and a team that is underperforming. Many organizations focus on the wrong way of incentivizing their team members with superficial techniques. Bonuses, commissions, employee benefits, and such incentives are all tactical ways to boost employee performances. They might work in the short term. However, only inclusive teams with inclusive leaders who listen and learn create a deep connection and engagement for each team member, resulting in a team willing to go above and beyond. Human beings are driven by their emotions; when an inclusive leader creates a deep sense of trust, respect, and connection, people will move mountains, including in the workplace.

Learning is the second important attribute of the inclusive leader. Many business leaders and organization leaders do not spend time learning from their team members. Regardless of excuses, including how busy/important/ unavailable they might be, leaders are missing out if they do not take the time to learn from their team members.

I once had a COO who, when he visited our regional office in London from his headquarters in San Francisco, took the time to meet with any employee who requested a meeting with him. In those one-to-one meetings, he would bring his notebook and his pen, and he would write things he heard in the meetings. When the American COO of a thousand employee company travels to regional offices in London and takes notes in his notebook during one-to-one meetings with individual contributors, it sends a strong message: the senior leadership team is willing to learn from its members in regional offices.

When an inclusive leader makes a point of learning from his team members, it also demonstrates a profound humility. Humble leaders who are willing to learn from their team members are more appreciated by their team members because they are showing that they are not above the group, but rather they are willing to learn and become better. This helps create a team that is more willing to learn and become better themselves because they can see their leader acting as a role model.

Learning is an essential attribute of inclusive leaders because it helps them become aware of things they did not know. It helps them understand their employees and even their market better, allowing them to become better leaders. On one occasion, my mentor Steve learned during our one-to-one that my team was building the plans for the next year without consulting the leaders of other departments on their projections. With that new knowledge, Steve took the action to speak to the wider team, allowing new plans for the following year to be aligned with all other departments. In that example, having a leader who took the time to listen and learn resulted in creating better plans for the business.

Learning comes with some very practical applications that actually improve the business and the organization.

The six characteristics of the inclusive leader. Paraphrasing a familiar adage, becoming an inclusive leader is a journey, not a destination. While it may seem like a long road and a daunting task to become an inclusive leader, the benefits that come with becoming an inclusive leader are many and extremely rewarding. During my career, I have observed six characteristics of inclusive leaders that I share with you in the following paragraphs.

1. Championing team members

In one of my previous roles, my mentor would say things such as "Perrine made a great point in that meeting." He used his privilege as a business leader to amplify my message, and he made me feel great. Inclusive leaders champion their team members by vocally supporting their work in all contexts but specifically in situations that will help those colleagues extend their reputation. Inclusive leaders can also talk about the experience they see in others, especially during performance reviews and promotion discussions. Champions can also recommend people for stretch assignments and new learning opportunities, and they can share a colleague's career goals with influencers within the organization.

Inclusive leaders sponsor their colleagues in public

ways. They refer team members in meetings and in visible, industry-wide events and conferences. They direct questions about specific topics to employees with subject matter expertise instead of answering themselves. They advocate for more women, people of color, and members of other underrepresented groups as keynote speakers and panelists at events. They recommend people from underrepresented groups when they are asked to speak at a conference or at an event, after asking them first if they'd like to speak.

2. Amplifying voices

Inclusive leaders use their voice to amplify the voices of their team members; they ensure that all voices are both heard and respected within the organization. Amplifying voices is focused on representing team members through communication. When someone proposes a good idea in a team meeting, inclusive leaders repeat it and give them credit: "I agree with Leila's recommendation for improving our Net Promoter Score." Inclusive leaders create a code of conduct for meetings. They invite members of underrepresented groups within the company to speak at staff meetings or to contribute to the company-wide newsletters or to take on other highly visible roles.

3. Advocating for others

Inclusive leaders use their power and influence to bring peers from underrepresented groups into exclusive circles. Inclusive leaders recognize and address unfair omissions, holding their peers accountable for including qualified colleagues of all genders, races and ethnicities, abilities, ages, religions, and sexual orientations. Inclusive leaders look closely at the invite lists for events, strategic meetings, important dinners with key partners, and other career building opportunities. When they see someone missing from a list, they advocate for them to be invited. Inclusive leaders introduce colleagues from underrepresented groups to influential people in their network. They ask colleagues from underrepresented groups to be co-authors or collaborators on important projects.

4. Studying and learning

Inclusive leaders always seek to learn as much as possible about the challenges faced by colleagues from underrepresented groups or any of their team members. Inclusive leaders do not insert their own personal opinions or experiences. Instead they simply listen and learn. They also don't expect colleagues from marginalized groups to provide research supporting that bias exists or to summarize best practices. Instead, inclusive leaders do their own research to seek out the relevant information. Inclusive leaders who seek to learn stay tuned in through publications, podcasts, social media by and about groups, and by asking co-workers about their experience. Inclusive leaders ask if they can join a Slack group representing an underrepresented group or if they can join an

Employee Resource Group for or by a certain group within their organization in order to learn and understand their peers better.

5. Speaking up

Inclusive leaders use their voice and their authority to speak up when necessary. They act as an upstander rather than as a bystander. The inclusive leader can see misconduct and act to address it. Inclusive leaders push back on offensive comments or jokes even if the targeted person or group is not in the room. Inclusive leaders always speak up when they see or hear speech that is degrading or offensive. They explain their stance so everyone is clear about why they are raising the issue. In meetings, inclusive leaders shut down off-topic questions that are asked only to test the presenter. Inclusive leaders take action if they see anyone in their organization being bullied or harassed. One way is to simply ask what is being discussed and check in with the victim privately.

6. Building trust and creating a safe space

Inclusive leaders make a point to create a safe space for all their colleagues to express their fears, frustrations, and needs. By simply listening to their colleagues' stories and by trusting that their colleagues are telling the truth, inclusive leaders create an important layer of support. Inclusive leaders don't assume something could not happen just because they haven't personally experienced it. Inclusive leaders listen and ask questions when someone describes an experience they have not experienced themselves. Inclusive leaders don't jump in with their personal stories. Inclusive leaders hold regular team meetings and encourage all team members to speak up about issues that are troubling them.

Inclusive leaders are human and therefore not perfect. They will make mistakes. The best inclusive leaders I have worked with were willing to risk making a mistake and to acknowledge when they were wrong. They also resisted getting defensive when being called out. Anyone can become an inclusive leader when they give themselves permission to make mistakes. By demonstrating that they are willing to acknowledge mistakes, inclusive leaders show that they are willing to learn to become a better inclusive leader.

Learning is an essential attribute of inclusive leaders because it helps them become aware of things they did not know.

9

COMMON INCLUSION PITFALLS TO AVOID

Most organizations do not have any inclusion program, and the few that do, do not have a robust inclusion program in place. Although inclusion is becoming an important topic of discussion among business leaders, it is still new to most and, therefore, it is often misunderstood and not implemented properly. In the spirit of helping you understand how to implement a successful inclusion framework for your organization, I have listed below and explained the seven most common inclusion practice mistakes that I have seen. It is important that you take the time to understand each of these most common inclusion program pitfalls and take note to avoid repeating them in your own organization.

1. Leaving out your corporate mission statement

When I worked with a London-based fintech startup on creating a diverse and inclusive team after they had acquired a smaller competitor, I quickly noticed that the company's mission statement had not been taken into consideration and more importantly, it did not mention inclusion or diversity. The startup leaders were focusing on short-term initiatives, including a series of diversity trainings and some speaking engagements on diversity and inclusion. None of the leadership team, line managers, or individual contributors had a clear vision of what the company's DNA was, and that was reflected in the tensions between departments and teams across the organization. Teams were not working well together, there were bottlenecks everywhere, and the leadership team was overwhelmed.

I recommended that we spend some time reviewing the corporate mission statement. The senior leadership team had a few meetings and came back to me after a few weeks with a brand new mission statement for the organization that focused on how diversity and inclusion were pillars of the organization. We quickly noticed some improvements in how teams worked together, especially after the CEO hosted a company-wide, all-hands meeting to share the new corporate mission statement and explain why diversity and inclusion were key pillars of the company's culture.

An organization's mission statement should include a clear, strong statement on the vision regarding these pillars. The company culture needs to be re-written at its core so that change happens at every level. The goal is to create a systemic culture of change. Crafting the corporate mission statement with a strong focus on diversity and inclusion is a key phase in the creation of a systematic process of change. The core values of the organization dictate what work is necessary.

At this stage, a culture of inclusion should be promoted often by the senior leadership team to all members of the organization. A greater sense of community will begin to emerge and employees will begin to come together from across all the different departments and will take part in creating tangible changes. The question should become how to sustain a culture of inclusion and incorporate the organizational core values in every facet of work and within the organization.

The success of this part of the systemic process is the responsibility of the senior leadership team as well as the HR department, hiring managers, and all line managers. Their mission is to make coworkers accountable for their behavior so that they continue the groundwork, and the culture of inclusion becomes woven into every facet of the organization.

2. Failing to get leadership commitment

Not getting the CEO's personal commitment on diversity and inclusion is probably the most common and deadly mistake of any inclusion program. Senior leadership support is one of the first requirements in creating a shared vision for a systemic change. Positive and lasting behavioral change is the primary requirement for a cultural change approach. Change agents must determine how new behaviors will become a strategic advantage for the success of the organization. These change agents are the senior leadership team members themselves because of their authority and influence within the organization. Diversity and inclusion have been perceived as separate concerns for too many years by members of the leadership team. The reality is that it takes the top leadership team of an organization to bridge the gap between good intentions and action. It is the vision and the personal commitment of the top leadership team that allows employees to be part of a behavioral process of culture change within the workforce and then makes them responsible for creating a long-lasting culture of inclusion.

3. Focusing on the short term only

Many organizations I have come across had a short-term vision of diversity and inclusion. A majority of them would host a diversity training, tick a box, and forget about diversity and inclusion for another twelve months. This leads to very little change in the organization, and this does not solve the inclusion challenges. As mentioned earlier, inclusion is a journey. Most successful organizations, such Apple and Google, have an ongoing diversity and inclusion program and are constantly challenging themselves on what they could do better. Best practices to ensure long-term success regarding diversity and inclusion include forming a D&I committee or taskforce, developing a strong diversity and inclusion mission statement that is shared often, executing regular internal diversity and inclusion surveys and training, and encouraging the CEO's regular participation in these initiatives.

4. Becoming complacent about your inclusion efforts

I have lost count of the times I have heard "we are doing great with our inclusion and diversity programs" statements from managers, mostly straight, white males, who were genuinely thinking that every employee in their organization was 100 percent engaged and felt 100 percent included at work. Like revenue and sales pipeline, inclusion is something that requires constant attention and effort. The most successful organizations are constantly investing time and resources in new, better inclusion programs. The best way to fail with diversity and inclusion programs is by being complacent and thinking that you are doing great. It is simply not good enough to bring in unconscious bias training, check a box, and think it is all done. I recommend that organizations set diversity and inclusion goals for their workforce composition, workforce composition in leadership, professional development, and leadership accountability and then constantly monitor the progress to assess where to invest next.

5. Failing to compensate for inclusion results

Another common mistake is to leave compensation or bonuses out of the diversity and inclusion conversation. If inclusion is good for business, then it should be compensated as such. Just like sales performance and marketing performance, inclusion performance should be rewarded as a business metric. Organizations that incentivize leaders by tying a certain percentage of their annual bonus to meeting specific diversity and inclusion goals set themselves up for success. As I mentioned earlier, I recommend 30 percent. The advantage of setting monetary rewards is that it drives real behavior in action. To drive a systemic culture of change, organizations must create goals that are linked with financial rewards.

6. Assigning inclusion to HR

Too many organizations still assign D&I to their HR department. The fact is, as soon as diversity and inclusion are passed on to HR, they get deprioritized, and this is where inclusion initiatives fail.

So why do business leaders assign diversity and inclusion to HR? There are multiple reasons for this. First is because it's convenient. As a busy CEO or managing director, the easy route is to delegate projects to other people. Most business leaders go into delegation mode as a way to cope with the number of responsibilities they carry. Delegation works and is even necessary for CEOs and managing directors to be able to scale the business. However the senior leadership team must take personal ownership of strategic projects. Delegating diversity and inclusion to HR means immediately deprioritizing the topic to "just another project."

Another reason why leaders delegate inclusion programs to HR is that they misunderstand diversity and inclusion. The common perception is that it is a charitable thing to do, a moral imperative, the right thing to do. Since diversity and inclusion are perceived as charitable projects, they get associated with "corporate social responsibility" and immediately passed on to HR to deal with it. D&I initiatives are not seen as the strategic business advantage they are.

Business leaders prioritize what they perceive as strategic, and they work on what they perceive as strategic business imperatives. Senior leadership teams prioritize sales forecast, strategic operations, and product launches, and usually anything else is delegated to other teams. When business leaders think of diversity and inclusion as a charitable thing to do, they prioritize it down the list to deliver their attention on what they believe is mission-critical to the business.

Finally, diversity and inclusion feel out of their comfort zone. Senior leadership teams feel overwhelmed by the very topics of D&I. Many CEOs would rather avoid the topics altogether and not get involved with them out of fear of saying the wrong thing or doing the wrong thing. It is a very common belief among CEOs and Managing Directors that diversity and inclusion are uncomfortable issues. They perceive them as difficult, perhaps political, and even embarrassing, so anything they can do to delegate these concerns to someone else will be done so they don't have to deal with the overwhelm.

Now that we've looked at why D&I is often assigned to HR, let's look at why assigning inclusion to HR is counterproductive. First, inclusion becomes tactical rather than a strategic business priority. The very instant diversity and inclusion are assigned to the HR department, they become HR projects instead of a strategic business goal. As a result, diversity and inclusion are not part of the daily agenda of the senior leadership team and are not part of any strategic plan. HR leaders start working in a silo from the senior leadership team, and there is no urgency, no momentum. This is where the initiative slowly starts to die on someone's desk.

Second, there is a lack of budget and authority that will slow down any inclusion initiative. HR simply lacks the budget and the authority to make the initiative successful. Assigning such initiatives to a department means the support it needs to become a strategic business initiative is missing, and it will become a side project, just like partnering with charities, that gets tactical wins at best and constantly gets deprioritized in most cases.

Assigning diversity to HR creates additional bottlenecks because each time a decision needs to be made, it has to go through a series of steps just to get approval, and this hinders any chance of significant advancement. This is part of the "deprioritization" of D&I initiatives. Like any other side project that is assigned to a specific department, it lacks the executive sponsorship it needs to make significant progress. The perception it creates as "just another HR project" immediately creates a lack of urgency, and the project simply won't get the attention it needs to be successful.

The question then becomes what to do instead of making the assignment to HR. First, as I have emphasized, organizations should assign inclusion programs to a senior leadership team member. Whether it is the CEO or the COO or the CRO, diversity and inclusion must be owned by one member of the senior leadership team. That business leader should have personal diversity goals that are tied to monetary compensation, and this should be at least 30 percent of their overall bonus. All senior leadership team members should also have diversity goals tied to their monetary compensation. This sends a clear message that diversity and inclusion are strategic business priorities, and the senior leadership team should treat them as such and make them part of regular discussions.

Second is creating that important D&I taskforce sponsored by an executive. This will ensure constant monitoring, evaluation, and improvement of the D&I initiatives. Having an executive leader on this taskforce will give the budget, the authority, and the resources needed to make an impact.

As discussed in chapter seven, you can choose the details of how many people are part of the taskforce, who will be in it, and how often they will meet. What is important is that the taskforce be sponsored by an executive and you clarify taskforce goals. These goals should be aligned with your diversity and inclusion goals. Finally, while HR should not be the owner of the inclusion initiatives, it should be a part of the initiative. HR leaders should provide input and feedback and be part of the regular meetings to discuss the progress of the initiatives. However, it is critical that the ownership of any D&I initiative remains with the senior leadership team executive at all times, so that the program is always treated as a strategic business goal and does not become a side project.

7. Failing to compensate inclusion and diversity partners appropriately

The year 2020 was a seismic year for diversity and inclusion issues. From Black Lives Matter to company diversity reports shared publicly to unconscious bias training galore, the social, political, and cultural events of 2020 created a new awareness of diversity and inclusion. Many organizations found a new interest in these topics, and some even started calling themselves diversity champions.

As more business leaders and organizations contacted me for my expert advice and speaking engagements on diversity and inclusion, I started noticing a pattern. Many organizations wanted a free ride! A significant number of professionals wanted me to work for free. So much so that I decided to write an article about this new phenomenon to expose the truth and raise awareness about this harmful trend. I called it "The rise of the free-rider diversity champion." Who are the free-rider diversity champions? What kind of behavior do they exhibit? Let's explore this free-rider approach that is symptomatic of how many organizations approach diversity.

Who are the free-rider diversity champions? As I received an increasing number of enquiries for my diversity services over the past few months, I was able to observe and recognize different types of free-rider diversity champions. Although they all want free diversity services, they belong to distinct groups that are worth discussing.

1. CEOs

This free-rider diversity champion typically is the CEO of a medium size organization and is after some free diversity advice. This individual contacts me on LinkedIn and asks for a free review of a new diversity policy or plan.

2. Senior leadership team members

They might be the Chief People Officer or the Chief Operations Officer of a medium size organization. They usually think they know everything about diversity and inclusion, and when they speak with me, the diversity expert, they like to tell me how to do diversity and inclusion. They don't listen. They are typically after tips and tactical advice they can use, although they are not willing to pay for it.

3. Managers or team leaders

This individual might be a team leader or a manager of a regional team in a large enterprise organization. They are usually extremely confident about their own outstanding diversity and inclusion skills as well as their organization's superb implementation of diversity. They absolutely believe they are doing everything perfectly fine when it comes to diversity and inclusion, yet they want me to give them free advice and tips on diversity best practices and share free insight on what other organizations are doing.

4. Conference program managers and event planners

They might be in charge of recruiting keynote speakers for their conference, or they might be recruiting speakers for a customer event. They claim that they absolutely value my work and my insight, yet they don't have any budget for me to speak about diversity and inclusion. They are usually genuinely expecting a free speaking engagement for their event and lay claim to be absolute diversity champions themselves.

What kind of behavior do these free-rider diversity champions exhibit? Not surprisingly they are looking for advice and support from their particular organization's concern. Here are four common requests:

1. A review

The most common request is for a free review and advice regarding their newly developed diversity policy and goals. They ask for a full analysis, evaluation, audit, and examination of their new diversity program, completely free of charge. As soon as I mention that this work will require payment, they tune out of the conversation.

2. A consultancy

The second most common request is for a free consultancy. In this case, the request is about how they should start their diversity program, which steps should come first, and what they should take into consideration. Often in this scenario, the request is also about a ton of insight into what other organizations are doing in the market to get a benchmark. Generally, the individual expects to have this work done completely free of charge.

3. A speaking engagement

In this scenario, the individual wants a free speaking engagement. They want a free keynote session or a free workshop on diversity and inclusion for their conference or for their customer event. They expect this work to be done completely free and claim that this will be good for the speaker because of the exposure and awareness. In the approach, they completely disregard the amount of work that goes into speaking.

4. Free content

> They ask for a free webinar, a free guide, or free content. This is a very common request from the free-rider diversity champion. They generally want free content to use for their customers. They are seeking free webinars, guides, and educational content on diversity and inclusion, so they can use it as a marketing asset to target their customers and prospects.

How is this free-rider approach harmful? In this free-rider diversity champion approach, the self-proclaimed diversity champions genuinely think of themselves as outstanding diversity champions. These individuals have a very strong belief that not only are they an outstanding ally and supporter of diversity and inclusion but also that they, in fact, act as a great ally because they are speaking with a diversity expert about their diversity idea. In their own mind, the free-rider diversity champion is doing a fantastic job with diversity and inclusion, and the diversity expert should feel lucky to be part of their project—as long as they don't charge for their work!

The free-rider diversity champion says that diversity is important but as soon as a budget is mentioned, they say that now is not the best time to focus on diversity and inclusion. They never prepare any budget for these initiatives, yet they firmly believe they are doing a great job with diversity and inclusion.

One danger of the free-rider diversity champion approach is that because they don't invest in D&I initiatives, they don't get the expertise they so desperately need, and they end up doing a poor job that is actually counterproductive and harmful to any D&I actions they might attempt. The free-rider diversity champion doesn't have any solid diversity program in place with goals and leadership involvement.

Another danger of the free-rider diversity champion approach is that this aligns with the wrong perception that diversity is a moral imperative and the right thing to do. This approach completely misunderstands how diversity is a secret, competitive advantage. This is counterproductive and harmful as this positions diversity the wrong way.

What should be done instead? It is becoming clear who truly takes action to support diversity and inclusion and who only talks about them and doesn't take any meaningful action. But the truth is that those self-proclaimed diversity champions are being recognized and exposed by the members of the public who are themselves more educated than ever before on these topics. Socially conscious and educated employees, stakeholders, customers, vendors, and members of the public now recognize those free-rider diversity champions and speak up about their lack of action. Smart leaders should take note now to avoid embarrassing situations for themselves and their organization.

If inclusion is
good for business,
then it should be
compensated as such.

10

PROMOTING A CULTURE OF INCLUSION IN REMOTE WORK

At the time of writing this book, the vast majority of organizations have adopted a remote work environment with companies like Facebook, Google, and Twitter announcing new policies that include permanent remote work settings. However, it is important to note that remote working comes with more disconnection and disengagement from employees.

Organizations are now and will continue to be faced with challenges related to lower employee engagement and lower employee productivity, which may lead to more employee turnover and lower employee morale. Below are some best practices I have learned in my career to foster a culture of inclusion during remote working.

Allow everyone to speak up. With Zoom meetings and conference calls becoming the new normal, it may be tough for some meeting participants to speak up, especially for those introverted personalities or those who were raised to wait for their turn to speak up. I think of women in particular here.

From poor internet connection to employees suffering from visual or hearing impairments, from introverted employees or those who wait for their turn to speak up, virtual meetings aggravate the gap between those who are more vulnerable and those who are more privileged. Appointing a moderator to keep time and to ask every participant to contribute in an equal manner is a great way to allow everyone to speak up equally. Creating new rules of engagement where participants can write their thoughts in advance to share before the meeting allows those introverted or visually impaired employees to share their ideas upfront. This is an effective way to share speaking time equally among all participants.

Be equitable. As an inclusive leader, you should work with your employees to create flexible work schedules that work for their needs. This could include finding solutions that work for carers (parents with young children, employees who care for relatives) and encouraging them to take extra days off to recharge mentally and physically. Revisit your leave plan and create policies that are equitable and helpful for the demands of today's lifestyle obligations. Take this opportunity to rewrite your leave policy and become the best-in-class company when it comes to employee benefits.

Create more opportunities for connection. As research shows,[1] minorities have been more impacted and challenged by COVID-19, so ensure that you create an environment that emphasizes connections between minority employees. Employee Resource Groups (ERG) are a very effective way to foster inclusion. Employee Resource Groups for women, parents, people of color, LGBT+, neurodiverse individuals, older workers, and younger workers are some very popular Employee Resource Groups that create connections among employees. These groups can create a deep sense of belonging and allow employees to bring their best selves to work every day even during remote working and COVID-19.

Accessible presentations. Accessibility is critical to allow every employee to feel included in the workplace. Ensure that all presentations in meetings use large fonts that are easy to read for everyone, offer a phone dial-in option for those hard of hearing or with poor internet connectivity, allow participants to turn off their camera to have better internet connection and hear the presentation, ensure that images used in presentations show diverse people and use inclusive language.

Remote working is giving organizations a sneak peek into the future of working. As an inclusive leader, you should leverage this opportunity to implement best practices to foster inclusion and allow each employee to feel included so they can bring their best selves to work every day.

Chapter 10 Notes

1. https://blogs.lse.ac.uk/politicsandpolicy/
    covid19-ethnic-minorities/

Creating new
rules of engagement
where participants can
write their thoughts
in advance to share
before the meeting
allows those introverted
or visually impaired
employees to share
their ideas
upfront.

11

ISOTROPIC SYSTEMS SUCCESS STORY

John Finney, CEO of Isotropic Systems, first spoke to me when his company was about to hire fifty new employees to sustain the rapid growth of his technology startup. During our first call, he talked about his vision for Isotropic Systems and how he wanted the company to become a role model and an example to follow at all levels. Diversity and inclusion were very important to him, and he needed some help to get there. We talked about how the technology industry has always struggled with diversity and inclusion, but we both wanted to focus on what could be done to establish Isotropic Systems as one of the most diverse and inclusive technology startups.

First, we discussed the need to create a D&I taskforce within the organization to monitor workforce inclusion and diversity progress. Then we announced to the company John's personal commitment to double female representation within 12 months. Finally, we created a diversity and inclusion training program with attendees including the entire leadership team, the HR team, and all line managers to create buy-in and awareness among the leadership teams.

In an interview I gave to DiversityQ, I explained that with only 17 percent of UK technology workers being female[1] and only 11 percent of senior leadership roles in technology being held by women,[2] the technology industry has long been recognized for its gender diversity problem. Beyond the underrepresentation of women, the gender pay gap also creates inequalities in technology. Men in high tech companies earn 25 percent more than women.[3]

As noted in chapter 7, "Only a quarter of start-ups (26 percent) are actively trying to increase diversity within their leadership teams," according to Silicon Valley Bank.[4] "Only 43 percent of startups surveyed said they had company-wide diversity goals, while fewer than one-in-five had these goals for executive positions. It is great to see a tech leader take on a personal commitment to set aggressive diversity goals."[5]

I worked closely with Isotropic Systems' top leadership team to articulate the business benefit of inclusion and diversity to further their commitment to the initiative. John explained, "We believe that attracting and retaining diverse employees will allow Isotropic Systems to be more innovative, to open up new markets, and to achieve greater productivity. We are committed to becoming a role model in the technology industry by leading by example. Being a finalist in the Microsoft Diversity in Tech Awards Cultural Inclusion category confirmed our commitment to diversity and inclusion."[6]

I personally believe that inclusive leaders like John make a difference in the world by taking action and being personally committed to bringing more diversity and inclusion in the workplace. It is my hope that more leaders will follow in John's footsteps and take action to create inclusive workplaces.

Chapter 11 Notes

1. https://digileaders.com/
   why-there-few-women-tech-reasons-positive/

2. https://www.mckinsey.com/industries/technology-
   media-and-telecommunications/our-insights/
   closing-the-tech-gender-gap-through-philanthropy-and-
   corporate-social-responsibility

3. https://www.uk.mercer.com/our-thinking/the-gender-pay-
   gap-in-uk-tech-sector.html#:~:text=Mercer%20has%20
   undertaken%20analysis%20of,the%20UK%20overall%20
   of%2018%25

4. https://www.weforum.org/agenda/2020/08/
   diversity-gap-startups-gender-ethnicity/

5. Ibid.

6. https://www.inspired-human.com/post/
   tech-startup-partners-with-d-i-expert-in-a-bid-to-drive-
   more-diversity-in-the-tech-sector

"We believe that attracting and retaining diverse employees will allow Isotropic Systems to be more innovative, to open up new markets, and to achieve greater productivity."

— John Finney, CEO of Isotropic —

12

TACKLING UNCONSCIOUS BIAS TO CREATE A CULTURE OF INCLUSION

Unconscious bias affects our decisions all the time, especially in the workplace. We like to think that we are objective, especially at work. In reality, we are all subject to unconscious bias, also known as implicit bias or hidden bias. The more we are aware of this, the more we can mitigate it. Unconscious bias at work has a significant negative impact on creating a culture of inclusion where each and every employee feels included, welcome, and like they belong. As you embark on your own journey to become an inclusive leader, you should take some time to understand the definition of unconscious bias and to really explore the impact it has in your own organization. You should also take note of the following suggestions to mitigate unconscious bias in the workplace.

What is unconscious bias? Unconscious bias is any

detectable bias in behavior or attitude that we are not ourselves aware of. It is as real and damaging as conscious prejudice and indeed can be more prevalent than other types of prejudice. Researcher Mike Noon of London's Queen Mary University defines it as "learned social stereotypes that are automatic, unintentional, deeply ingrained, universal and able to influence behavior.[1] One landmark piece of research carried out at Yale and Washington universities in a 1998 study found that some form of bias runs through up to 95 percent of people.[2] There are a number of examples of unconscious bias in the workplace.

Gender Bias

A common unconscious bias example in this situation is referred to as "bropropriating." This occurs when a female member of the team makes a point about something and there isn't much interest in it. Then, a short time later, a male member of the team makes the same point, and everyone supports it. This bias can lead to female workers not wanting to share their ideas and can be an incredibly frustrating and demotivating factor.

Name Bias

This unconscious bias example comes into play most often when choosing people to interview. Despite best intentions, managers can be biased when reading names they consider "foreign." This is obviously an issue as it can inhibit growth in diversity and preclude many qualified applicants from being interviewed.

Similarity Bias

The similarity bias essentially states that we like working with people similar to us. This could be graduates from specific schools, people who have worked at certain companies, and more. Organizations that are influenced by the similarity bias run the risk of having no diversity among their ideas and perspectives, which could lead to less-than-ideal solutions to problems.

The Halo Effect

The halo effect, sometimes called the halo error, is the tendency for positive impressions of a person to reflect positively or influence judgments and opinions in other areas. For example, when reading a prospective candidate's CV, you may see that they went to a particular university and this may influence your opinions positively when looking at other areas, especially those that they may fall down on.

The Horns Effect

The horns effect is essentially the opposite of the halo effect. It is an unconscious bias that causes the perception of an individual to be unfairly influenced by a single negative trait. For example, if an individual uses a particular phrase that we don't like, we may subsequently begin disliking a lot of things they say as a result.

Confirmation Bias

Another common example of unconscious bias is confirmation bias. This exists not only at work, but in everyday life as well. Confirmation bias occurs when we make a decision about something, then actively look for information that supports that decision, while overlooking any opposing facts and viewpoints. This can be detrimental to the success of an organization because it follows pre-conceived ideas that have not been objectively researched prior to being executed.

Age Bias

Age bias occurs when assigning tasks to people based on their age. A common example would be a tech-heavy project. The unconscious bias may cause a manager to assume that a younger person would be more apt to handle this job better than an older one. In this case, assuming one's experience or proficiency is based entirely on an opinion that isn't backed up by fact is a perfect example of unconscious bias. After all, many older people are technologically savvy, so it would be unfair to assume they wouldn't be right for the job.

What impact can unconscious bias have at work? Just like racism in its more overt forms, unconscious bias has a strongly negative impact on relationships in the workplace and hinders career growth for some. It may also adversely affect decisions on recruitment and impair diversity.

A study by the British Academy conducted in early 2019, for example, found a strong name bias in recruitment. On average, nearly a quarter (24 percent) of white British applicants got positive replies from employers, while just 15 percent of ethnic minority candidates with the same applications got positive responses.[3] Unconscious bias perpetuates racism and other discriminations in the workplace, and, if not tackled, it will prevent any anti-racism work from taking place or the creation or existence of any diverse and inclusive workplace.

What can be done about unconscious bias in the workplace? There are various ways of tackling unconscious bias in the workplace, but awareness of it is a crucial first step, particularly among decision-makers. Colleagues could monitor one another and challenge any remarks or reinforcing of stereotypes, or a diversity and inclusion committee could be established. Equally, it may well be worth revisiting the rationale behind some recent decision (hiring, promoting) to see if any bias of which you were unaware at the time could have crept in.

At the same time, try and make slower, more considered decisions rather than snap decisions. Implementing processes for decision-making including hiring, promoting, and nominating can help reduce bias by forcing the decision-maker to think before making decisions. You also need to think about how best to educate your staff on this type of prejudice and its potential negative impact.

What is unconscious bias training? Unconscious bias training in the workplace is aimed at exposing employees to discrimination taking place that they may not be aware of. Such programs work to shift people's automatic thinking patterns and responses, ultimately to help eliminate discriminatory behavior altogether. The idea is to make people more aware of where they are most likely to make implicit associations and how to stop themselves from making such connections so they will not impact others. For example, reading about a Muslim terrorist and then having the word "terrorist" come into your brain next time you hear the word "Muslim."

Over the last 10 years or so, organizations including Starbucks, Facebook, and Google have increasingly introduced this training in a bid to enhance their diversity and inclusion programs. Almost all Fortune 500 businesses and most of the FTSE 350 now implement such programs.

Starbucks famously closed thousands of its US outlets for an afternoon to conduct racial bias training after a staff member in Philadelphia called the police just because two Black men sat down in the store without ordering anything.

Are there any potential downsides to unconscious bias training? In a word, yes. Bad training, for instance, doesn't just fail to work, it can be actively counterproductive. Equally, it won't work if it's seen as a "quick fix" or complete solution. And no one should come away afterwards thinking that such bias is not their fault because it's unconscious or feeling they have no personal responsibility for the damage it can cause. Another potential downside is that with this type of training it is sometimes hard to measure accurately to assess its impact. Finally, clearly conscious bias needs to be tackled at the same time as unconscious bias to create a holistic approach.

Chapter 12 Notes

1. https://www.emerald.com/insight/content/doi/10.1108/HRMID-05-2018-0102/full/html

2. https://www.theguardian.com/uk-news/2018/dec/02/unconscious-bias-what-is-it-and-can-it-be-eliminated

3. https://www.personneltoday.com/hr/study-finds-alarming-discrimination-against-minority-ethnic-candidates/

**There are
various ways
of tackling
unconscious bias
in the workplace,
but awareness of it
is a crucial first step,
particularly among
decision-makers.**

13

6 SIMPLE WAYS TO GET UNCONSCIOUS BIAS TRAINING RIGHT IN YOUR WORKPLACE

As discussed earlier, unconscious bias training has become increasingly more widespread. The majority of organizations contacting me want to have unconscious bias training first and foremost. There are different reasons why companies ask for unconscious bias training. Some organizations want to have this training to respond to the recent #blacklivesmatter movement. Organizations need to respond to this movement in a meaningful way that goes beyond just making a new pledge on their website. Many organizations need unconscious bias training as a first step to responding to this movement.

Some organizations want to host unconscious bias training to respond to non-white employees who are demanding more actions. Many organizations have mentioned that some non-white employees are vocal about how they feel, and they demand to see more meaningful actions from their employers to address the lack of equal opportunities and unequal representation as well as to give a meaningful response to Black Lives Matter.

Some organizations want to host unconscious bias training in order to address a very homogeneous workplace. Many companies want to address their own lack of workforce diversity as well as address the lack of workforce diversity in the organizations they invest in. Recently, a London-based VC contacted me to get trained on unconscious bias to diversify their workforce, which is white male dominated, and, more importantly, to ensure that as VCs, they will invest in startups that are founded by women and people of color.

Finally, some organizations want to host a company-wide unconscious bias training in order to mitigate and prevent micro-aggressions and discrimination.

Unconscious bias training offers the many D&I benefits to business that we've mentioned: attracting and retaining diverse talent by removing implicit bias, getting a greater diversity of thought, and opening up to new market opportunities. Discovering more revenue streams by better understanding the customer base, building better products to increase revenue and customer retention, increasing employee engagement and productivity, and keeping a competitive edge are also among the benefits of removing unconscious bias in the workplace.

While there is controversy on whether unconscious bias training is effective, I've indicated, in my experience, unconscious bias training is effective when it is done the right way because it offers the benefits named above. Here are six ways to get unconscious bias training right in your organization:

1. **Get the right content to the right audience with the right context.**

   This is going to sound familiar, but it bears repeating. Unconscious bias training should structure the content around real life workplace situations rather than science and research. The content should be action-oriented and should provide plenty of practical exercises for participants as well as workplace related assignments. Top leadership including the CEO should attend the training to fully understand what it is, buy into it, and commit to being held accountable for proactively fighting unconscious bias at the organizational level. Unconscious bias training must explain why it is important and how it ties to real business outcomes and to the business mission. As with any D&I training, unless the organization clearly articulates how this training ties to a business outcome, it will fail.

2. **Evaluate the impact of the training.**

   By measuring employee engagement and belonging before and after the unconscious bias training, the

organization ensures that the impact of the training goes beyond just the week of the training and
is measured and evaluated on an ongoing basis after
training. Measuring the results of unconscious bias
training isn't helpful unless you utilize the learnings to
improve your workplace processes. Evaluate any bias
or diversity training using the same five questions:

- How did the participants react or respond to the
  training?

- What did participants learn from the training?

- Did the trainees take what they learned and put it into
  on-the-job practice?

- Did the training meet the stakeholders' expectations?

- What was the return on these expectations (ROE)?

**3. Appoint a diversity taskforce sponsored by an
executive.**

Many organizations that have succeeded with diversity and inclusion, including fighting unconscious
bias, have created that diversity and inclusion taskforce I have often referred to in this book, whose
role is to regularly measure and evaluate the progress
made in regard to diversity and inclusion (and thus
unconscious bias) and who will speak up when no
progress is made. Remember, there must be executive
sponsors on this taskforce for it to be successful. The
goal is to monitor and improve the organization's

D&I initiatives. If your taskforce is made up of volunteers who have a personal interest in the topic and who will drive this initiative forward, it will have a greater success.

4. Follow-up with goal setting exercises to drive behavior.

As already pointed out, in order to translate positive intentions into measurable actions, the organization must set goals tied to monetary bonuses for the leadership team. These goals will hold leaders accountable and drive behavior. Make sure that your organization treats these goals the same way they treat sales goals and financial goals. I recommend that your CEO personally takes part in the goal setting exercise in order to have their full commitment. At this stage, you may need to remind your CEO of these significant statistics presented in chapter seven: inclusive organizations are **twice** more likely to exceed financial targets (Deloitte Research),[1] and that 85 percent of CEOs whose companies have an inclusiveness strategy said it's improved their bottom line (PWC CEO Survey).[2]

In my experience, 90 percent of companies will not implement a sustainable, long-term diversity program. Make your organization part of the 10 percent group!

5. Make the training voluntary and repeatable.

The unconscious bias training should be voluntary

because any mandatory training could create ill will and pushback. Employees are usually willing to participate provided companies let them know that the program is important. Explain to employees why and how they will benefit from this training. In other words, what's in it for them.

Employees know that they need to learn new things to stay relevant in the job they have and to prepare for future opportunities. Ask managers to support training efforts. Managers should want employees to attend training and keep their skills fresh. Hold managers and employees accountable for content. Instead of holding people accountable for attending a training program, hold them accountable for practicing the content. Make the training repeatable. As with any D&I training, I recommend continued training every three months. This allows maximized impact and keeps participants focused on unconscious bias.

6. Embed the training as part of a larger approach to diversity.

To refresh your memory from previous chapters, it's important to understand why diversity is significant to your organization. Whatever the reason is for what makes diversity and inclusion an important value for your organization, you must take the time to craft your answer, clearly articulate why that's important, and write it down.

How does diversity tie to your mission? Once you have done the work of articulating why D&I is important to your organization, you must work on how D&I ties to your mission. This is your opportunity to revisit or even create from scratch your organization's mission statement. We've touched on the importance of this already. Your mission statement defines what your organization is, why it exists, and its reason for being. At a minimum, your mission statement should define who your customers are and identify your products and services. At this stage, you must work on articulating how diversity and inclusion are part of your organization's mission statement. When you describe your organization's reason for being, you must clearly articulate how diversity and inclusion are part of your mission.

This is probably the most critical part of setting your organization for success regarding D&I initiatives, so take time to do this. If possible, try to tie in why your organization exists with a diversity and inclusion statement. It might sound like: "Our mission is to give free access to education to everyone because we believe that universal education will make the world more inclusive and bring more diversity in the workplace, in public institutions, and in academia." Or here's another one: "Our business exists because we believe everyone deserves always-on access to services regardless of their gender, race, socio-economic background, sexual orientation, age, and any other background." Write it down in your mission statement and share your new mission statement everywhere: on your website, on your social media, with your employees, in a newsletter to your clients, in the news. Print your new mission statement and place it somewhere you and your team can see it every day.

Additional initiatives beyond just unconscious bias training are also required to create a meaningful, long-term commitment to diversity and inclusion. Face the truth about how diverse your workplace is or is not. At this point, as you get started with your own D&I programs, begin with a look at your own workforce diversity and inclusion. Measure how diverse and inclusive your workforce is today so that you can track progress on your organization's D&I journey.

Limit defensiveness while communicating the importance of managing bias. I've spoken about defensiveness already and mention it again because it can be a real factor in your initiative's efforts. You now know that a common response to unconscious bias training, or any diversity and inclusion training, is defensiveness so you know to make sure that the training is positioned in a way to defuse that defensiveness by clearly articulating the benefits D&I will bring to your workplace.

Be a change agent. Your support, commitment, and accountability are essential elements to the implementation of a systematic process of inclusion at the workplace. Be the change you wish to see in your organization without expecting anyone else to do the work for you. As you become more and more accountable for becoming inclusive, you will see a snowball effect with an increasing number of peers, colleagues, and partners who follow in your footsteps. Do not get discouraged if you do not see immediate changes. You are planting the seeds of change. You will see results as you persevere.

As we transition into a new way of working where employees are more aware of social inequities, organizations must proactively take meaningful action to prevent unconscious bias and to boost diversity and inclusion. A Paychex study shows that 75 percent of employees are more loyal to highly transparent businesses.[3] Organizations will need to be more transparent in regard to their diversity and inclusion initiatives. According to a Fisher Phillip study, June 2020's employee lawsuits increase represented an "exponential" rise in case filings. The study found discrimination and work-from-home or leave claims dominated the collection, representing 63 and 62 of the total cases, respectively.[4] The pace of employee litigation has been accelerating. As employees are more likely to sue their employers for discrimination, organizations will need to invest more in unconscious bias training and in diversity and inclusion training to mitigate related workplace issues.

Chapter 13 Notes

1. https://www2.deloitte.com/content/dam/insights/us/articles/4209_Diversity-and-inclusion-revolution/DI_Diversity-and-inclusion-revolution.pdf

2. https://www.pwc.com/gx/en/diversity-inclusion/best-practices/assets/the-pwc-diversity-journey.pdf

3. https://www.paychex.com/articles/human-resources/effect-of-employer-transparency

4. https://www.fisherphillips.com/resources-alerts-fp-covid-19-employment-litigation-tracker-reveals

Your support, commitment, and accountability are essential elements to the implementation of a systematic process of inclusion at the workplace.

14

LEVERAGING DIVERSITY AND INCLUSION TRAINING TO CREATE A CULTURE OF INCLUSION

Beyond unconscious bias training alone, diversity and inclusion trainings are very effective tools to create a culture of inclusion that fosters engagement, productivity, and ultimately, performance. However, while most business leaders are very familiar with sales strategy, operations management, and people operations, very few senior leadership teams know about diversity and inclusion or even diversity training.

Considering the significant social changes that are reshaping our society, it is becoming inevitable for today's business leaders to deal with diversity and inclusion as part of their roles as leaders, and they need to prepare for it. The reality is that many leaders are unsure how to choose a diversity partner, what diversity training entails, or even why diversity training needs to be done in the first place. I have collected information here to give you a definitive guide for business leaders to choose the right diversity training for their organization.

What is diversity training and why does it matter? Diversity training is an initiative taken by organizations to create awareness of diversity and inclusion and achieve greater team collaboration and engagement. It is often a part of the leadership development programs and focuses on levelling the playing field for all. Organizations and business leaders often misunderstand the real value of a diversity training that's done right for their organization. As has been discussed and examples given, diversity and inclusion training programs can promote business performance, productivity, and growth.

Boston Consulting Group research revealed that over a quarter of employees at large companies do not feel that their direct manager is committed to diversity and inclusion.[1]

Here are the most important questions business leaders should ask when choosing diversity training for their organization.

What business benefits does the diversity and inclusion training offer? As a business leader, you should make sure that the diversity training offers real, tangible business benefits for your organization. The diversity and inclusion training's benefits should be clearly articulated by the diversity consultant and should include:

- attracting and retaining top talent by removing bias in hiring, giving feedback, and promoting. The training should help attract more diverse candidates and create a more inclusive culture where diverse talents thrive, are promoted, and feel engaged and valued.

- promoting a greater diversity of thoughts. A good diversity training should ultimately boost creative thinking and innovation in your organization because it will teach leaders how to attract and retain diverse talents who will see things in a variety of ways and from different perspectives.

- understanding your customer base better by educating leaders on creating an inclusive work environment. A better understanding of your diverse customer base will help you build better products and services that sell well and increase revenue, customer retention, customer satisfaction, and your Net Promoter Score.

- increasing employee engagement and productivity. Teaching companies how to mitigate unconscious bias and microaggressions, preventing biased language and discriminations, and reinforcing good diversity training will make all employees feel more included and engaged, increasing the productivity of the organization.

- making better decisions. By teaching all leaders and employees how to effectively work together, a good diversity training will help build teams that are better at solving difficult problems faster.

What systems are used to make the diversity training effective? Business leaders should ask their diversity and inclusion consultant questions about what specific systems would be used to maximize the effectiveness of the training. Here are some questions and answers to look for.

- **Is the content action-oriented?** The topics covered in the diversity training should include real workplace scenarios that all employees can relate to and should provide many practical examples and exercises that every employee will immediately recognize and be able to use in their day-to-day work.

- **Who should be included in the training?** The audience of the diversity training should include the leadership team. The top leadership of the organization, including the CEO, should attend the diversity training in order to fully understand what it is, buy into it, and commit to being held accountable for proactively fighting unconscious bias at the organizational level.

- **How should our organization position D&I training?** The diversity training should be part of a diversity strategy and be positioned as one of the initiatives that the organization is undertaking to promote diversity and inclusion. The diversity consultant should work hand in hand with the business leaders to articulate to all employees why this is important and how it ties to real business outcomes and to the business mission. Unless the diversity consultant works closely with the business leaders and clearly articulates how the diversity training ties to real business outcomes, the initiative won't be successful.

- **Will we see measurable results from this training?** The training impact must be evaluated. By measuring employee engagement before and after the diversity training, the diversity consultant and the organization will ensure that the impact of the training goes beyond just the week of the training and is measured and assessed over a longer period of time.

- **How are the D&I initiatives managed after the training?** A diversity and inclusion taskforce must be created. Many organizations that have succeeded with diversity and inclusion, including fighting unconscious bias, use a diversity and inclusion taskforce to regularly measure and evaluate the progress achieved. The taskforce must speak up when no progress is made. The executive sponsors on this taskforce must fully support the work for the initiative to be successful.

- **How do we measure the impact of the training?** There must be follow-up with goal setting exercises to drive behavior. In order to translate positive intentions into measurable actions, the diversity consultant should work with you to set goals tied to monetary bonuses for the leadership team. These goals should hold leaders accountable and drive behavior.

- **Should we make this training mandatory for all employees?** The training should be voluntary, not mandatory. The diversity consultant should advise you to make the diversity training voluntary to prevent or reduce any counter-productive impact.

- **Is this a one time, standalone training?** The diversity training should be made repeatable over time. I recommend every three months to keep the awareness top of mind and to ensure that the impact of the training is long-lasting.

- **Are there other actions to consider with ongoing D&I Initiatives?** The diversity training should be embedded as part of a larger approach to tackle unconscious bias and diversity and inclusion. For example, the diversity consultant might recommend such things as any employee who takes part in the hiring process reads some common bias behaviors before interviewing. Setting diversity and inclusion goals for the leadership team tied to monetary bonuses is important as I have emphasized.

- **What if we get pushback from employees when we announce this training?** There must be a balance between limiting defensiveness about diversity training and communicating the importance of diversity training. Positioning for this training is critical and that means clearly articulating the benefits that will come from it.

- **What industry events has the diversity consultant spoken at and what industry credentials can they share?** When choosing a diversity consultant to deliver your diversity training, you want a professional with experience relevant to your business. Business leaders should enquire about any industry recognition and credentials held by the consultant. A good diversity consultant should be a frequent contributor to the industry and regularly educate the market on diversity best practices through public speaking, contributing articles, podcasts, videos, and more. Ask the diversity consultant if they have been involved with any diversity awards, such as the diversity in tech awards[2] as part of the judging panel, or by partnering with any sponsor. Ask the diversity consultant what industry event they speak at regularly, what publications they contribute to, and what kind of content they share on diversity and inclusion to educate the market on diversity best practices. Diversity publications such as DiversityQ and Fair Play Talks should feature your diversity consultant. If your diversity partner is really committed to creating a more diverse, inclusive society, they should contribute to diversity education outside of just their clients.

- **What type of organizations have they provided diversity and inclusion training for?** Diversity consultants should be willing to share references and customer reviews and business leaders should ask for these references. A good diversity consultant should have helped organizations similar to yours.

Ideally, they should share customer references of organizations similar to yours, from the same industry, and of a similar size. Your diversity consultant should be able to make introductions with business leaders and HR professionals they have worked with so you can ask for references. You should also search for online reviews to check the reputation of your diversity consultant.

Choosing the right diversity training for your organization can feel like a daunting task, especially for business leaders who might feel outside of their comfort zone in this arena. However, as social changes become more and more part of our society and business leaders are expected to take action to promote diversity and inclusion, senior leadership teams must educate themselves to understand what's needed. By asking simple questions when seeking a diversity consultant, leaders can select the right partner to deliver the most effective diversity training for their organization. Take the first step to promote diversity and inclusion in your organization today by booking a diversity and inclusion discovery call: https://www. inspired-human.com/contact.

Chapter 14 Notes

1. https://www.bcg.com/publications/2020/
   frontline-leaders-make-break-progress-diversity

2. https://diversityintechawards.online/

As social changes
become more and more
part of our society,
and business leaders
are expected
to take action to
promote diversity
and inclusion,
senior leadership teams
must educate themselves
to understand
what's needed.

15

HOW TO BE MORE INCLUSIVE OF WOMEN IN THE WORKPLACE

At the time of writing this book, COVID-19 is still affecting all countries around the world. As we have seen in the media, decades of workplace gender equality progress is under threat since the beginning of COVID-19. Research shows that women have been struggling to strike a balance with childcare, homeschooling, and housework more than men have since the beginning of the pandemic in March 2020. Research has also indicated that the paid hours worked by women who are still employed have plummeted by half more than for men, with women cutting back their hours by 11.5 percent as compared with 7.5 percent for male employees.[1] These statistics are concerning, and there is a huge cultural shift that needs to happen to stop reversing the efforts of bridging the gender gap in recent years.

We know that things like diversity and inclusion programs tend to go backwards during recessions and crises. With women dropping out of the labor market in disproportionately high numbers,[2] there is a danger that some of them will be locked out of work for good. Women are more targeted by redundancy and furlough schemes than men, partly because they tend to be in more junior positions and partly because of unconscious bias associated with women as being the main caregiver at home. Women are also the majority of workers in healthcare, education, and social services, and these sectors have been hit hard by COVID-19.

Is the next generation of women setback? Can anything be done to reverse the gender gap? Thankfully there are some practical steps that can be implemented by organizations to bridge the gender gap in the workplace during COVID-19.

Reskill women for employment in high growth sectors. Even before COVID, structural shifts that were increasing demand for particular skills were underway. Technological progress was expected to bring significant change in demand for particular roles in the workforce. Demand for Information and Communication Technology (ICT) specialists as well as for "future skills" are rising. Demand is expected to decline for administrative roles. Companies must retrain and future-proof their female workforce by offering training focusing on ICT skills and other skills on the rise to show their commitment to bridging the gender gap.

Partner with local authorities and government. Organizations should seek support from the government and local authorities to create incentives that will help reshape economies to be more equitable for women. In return for financial support—such as tax rebates—during the crisis, governments can require businesses to invest in training and upskilling their female workforce.

Review support for mothers in the workplace. Organizations should offer childcare support for working mothers including financial contributions to childcare and flexible working hours. Companies must ensure they provide adequate pumping space for new mothers. Organizations should encourage a community for working mothers by creating a working mother Employee Resource Group (ERG) and a Slack channel. These "working mother" communication channels will be a valuable resource where working mothers can connect, share resources and tips, and find community support while working.

Businesses should also update their parental leave policy. Leading tech companies such as Netflix have extended their parental leave policies in order to retain and attract top talent. Companies should review their plan to reintegrate new mothers. By offering reduced hours during the first few months after childbirth and by communicating with mothers-to-be and current mothers, organizations can create a better working environment to better meet the needs of working mothers.

Promote women into leadership positions. By setting goals for women in leadership positions, organizations show a real commitment in action to bridge the gender gap. Ideally, the leadership team should have such goals that are assessed during performance reviews and attached to bonuses and promotions. A meaningful goal that will achieve equal representation in leadership positions should be 50 percent of the leadership being female. This metric should be assessed on a monthly basis and actions should be implemented to move the organization toward that goal.

Chapter 15 Notes

1. https://newsroom.kpmg.com.au/
    gender-impacts-covid-19-budget-update/

2. https://www.theguardian.com/business/
    commentisfree/2020/may/17/despite-the-horror-of-
    australias-unemployment-numbers-we-havent-reached-
    the-bottom-yet

We know that things like
diversity and inclusion
programs tend to go
backwards during
recessions and crises.

16

HOW TO BE MORE INCLUSIVE OF BLACK COLLEAGUES IN THE WORKPLACE

As the world has been experiencing a pandemic of racism at the time of writing this book, especially following the tragic death of George Floyd in the United States, many business leaders and companies are looking for ways to support their Black colleagues. As an inclusive leader, it is an important part of your journey to support Black colleagues and people of color, especially during a pandemic of racism. Here are some practical tips you can use to better support these colleagues.

Make a strong company statement. The leadership team of your organization should make a strong public statement to speak up against racism and show their commitment to proactively end racism. Employees should proactively push their leadership teams to be vocal about their statement against racism and against discrimination at work. This is a corporate social responsibility, and it will have a positive impact on communities and society if done in a correct way.

Donate to relevant charities. Donate money or time to causes that further educate on and take action to end racism. Whether it is at the organizational level or at the individual level, everyone should donate what they can to support organizations that fight to end racism.

Proactively ask your Black colleagues how they wish to be supported. Practicing empathy and offering support to your Black colleagues should be emphasized. If managers don't acknowledge the emotional impact on their colleagues and employees during an international crisis, they will not be prepared to address the implications that has for their company's bottom line.

Speak up. Speak up, stand up, say something. Remaining silent in instances of racism is being complicit. Speaking up will help the company and society move toward equality. Too many organizations remained silent during the social events of 2020. Too many company leaders also took little to no stance in regard to the events that unfairly targeted Black individuals in 2020. Leaders have an obligation to speak up and to take a stance against racism. Silence is not an option for inclusive leaders.

Listen and learn. Listen and acknowledge your colleague's feelings. Don't talk. Focus on listening and learning without judgment. Listening and learning help foster workplace inclusion, creating an atmosphere where all employees belong, contribute, and thrive. It requires deliberate and intentional action. As we discussed earlier, active listening is about focusing on what the person is saying without the intent to reply. Listening fully can be one of the strongest actions you can take to support your Black colleagues at work.

Actively hold your managers and colleagues accountable. Employees should hold their leadership team accountable for their actions. Employees should report any instances of racism, regardless of how small they might seem. Be the person who brings up the topic of how to better support Black colleagues at work during meetings. Do not be the person who remains silent and who doesn't ask for updates on what the organization is doing to support Black colleagues.

Mentor Black colleagues. Managers should be encouraged to identify talent within teams and to support them with the knowledge and opportunity to succeed. Managers should offer Black mentees stretch assignments and glamour work, speak of them positively when they are not in the room, and ask them what their career goals are. Becoming an ally to Black colleagues is a critical response to racism and discrimination in the workplace. Mentoring Black colleagues enforces a behavior of equity in the organization and works toward fair outcomes for Black colleagues by treating them in ways that address their unique barriers.

Read. Employees and managers should proactively read

books and articles and listen to podcasts to educate themselves about the history of systemic racism across the world to help them better understand what is happening today. Actively seeking to become more educated on the topic of Black individuals, Black culture, and Black people in the workplace will open up new perspectives and help a better understanding of what Black colleagues might be experiencing.

Create new communication channels. Creating a new Slack channel or company forum specifically on the topic of racism will help fight racism and educate about racism. Invite as many colleagues as possible to become active members of that channel. This will educate colleagues who might have unconscious bias against Black individuals.

Becoming an inclusive leader means that you actively seek ways to better support all your team members, especially those from under-represented groups as they need additional support to feel included, valued, and welcome.

17

CHANGE STARTS WITH YOU

Today, leaders around the world will do something remarkable. A regional VP at a software company will finally speak to that disruptive team member who tells jokes that make everyone feel uncomfortable and give him a final warning. A CEO of a public company will fire her head of sales, who has been known for bullying her team members and for being rude and disrespectful to her colleagues. A marketing director will finally speak up about the abusive relationship her boss has been creating and give a final warning to her management that she will no longer tolerate bullying at work.

Initially, each of these people will feel scared and worried, but they are going to do it anyway because they knows this cannot continue. These leaders know they might not be popular, and they might risk their jobs, but they also know this is the right thing to do, and so they will do it.

These leaders know what it takes to be an inclusive leader, and they are ready and willing to be the change. Most people spend the majority of their waking hours in a job. Working in an environment that is inclusive, respectful, and safe is not a luxury. It is a necessity. Leaders have a fantastic position in the organization to be the change, and when they know what the right thing to do is, they do it. Becoming an inclusive leader is a choice.

These leaders who are going to do something remarkable today also know the alternative. It would mean dealing with inappropriate colleagues who keep bullying the team with their inappropriate jokes and their depreciation humor every day. Dealing with that toxic head of sales after receiving report after report of bullying and misconduct by different employees who have been treated with disrespect and threats. Dealing with a bully every day who makes coworkers feel like they are not worthy and thereby causing their mental, emotional, and physical pain.

Leading with a blind eye to all the things that need to be addressed in the organization and pretending that toxic situations in the team do not exist are no longer options for these inclusive leaders. The greatest risk for these leaders is to go through their life without being the leader they want to be.

The marketing director who will speak up about her toxic boss and give a final warning is scared but she knows this is how she wants to be as a leader, so she will do it anyway. Once she does this, she will feel better, and she will be on her way to becoming the inclusive leader she always wanted to be. Whatever happens next, she is on the right path, and she will continue to push herself to be the change she always wanted to see in organizations.

The VP of sales who will find the courage to speak to that toxic team member will finally feel like he is being true to the kind of leader he wants to be. Although it will be a difficult conversation and he might get some pushback further along the line, he is on his way to becoming the inclusive leader that he always wanted to be, and he feels, for the first time in a long time, like he is on the right leadership path. His confidence as a leader will start growing and positive changes in his team will start to show.

The CEO of the public company who will finally fire that toxic head of sales is also following her instinct as an inclusive leader to push through her discomfort and her fears about firing such a senior executive in her team. She will do it, and she will start to feel like she is on her way to becoming a better leader and creating a better team that focuses on respect, trust, and connections. She knows that this is the beginning of a new chapter in her organization where employees are more connected to each other, more engaged with their work, and more productive.

What the marketing director, the VP of sales, and the CEO of the public company have in common is a desire to become the leader they always wanted to be and to become the inclusive leader they always knew they were. What they also have in common is the newfound feeling of doing the right thing, and they will also discover that once they push through their initial fear of changing, the fear will disappear.

For these three leaders, it took the worst situation in their team to start the change they had postponed. But once they pushed through their initial fears and discomfort, they started becoming the change, and they began their journey to become an inclusive leader.

I shared these three stories at a speech recently, and Paul was in the audience. Paul came up to me after my talk, and he said that the story of the CEO had hit him close to his heart. Paul thanked me and said my talk was the highlight of the conference for him. He explained he was the CEO of a company himself and that he had been dealing with one senior executive in particular who has been known in the company for being disrespectful with some team members, for being difficult to deal with, and for creating a very toxic environment for her team. Since she was one of the longest established members of the leadership team and had joined the company before he became the CEO, he had always felt she was untouchable. The atmosphere in the company had become so bad that some senior executive team members wouldn't work with her at all. He added he got reports of misconduct by her almost every week from his HR department. He said that hearing me talk about the CEO of the public company today and the decision the CEO made to become an inclusive leader really struck a chord with him, and he felt that now was the time for him to address the situation in his organization.

We spoke about the best leaders we had in our careers, and I spoke about my mentor, Steve. We spoke about how Steve would always use his position as a leader to address any situation that needed to be addressed and how that created the type of inclusive environment that everyone wants to work in. Paul closed our conversation when he said, "It's time for me to change. I've been lying to myself by pretending I could ignore the situation. Today, I'm making the decision to be the inclusive leader I always wanted to be, to honor my team members, who are being bullied, harassed, or treated less than they need to be treated. Thank you so much, I will be sharing this."

Like Paul, you can be the change you wish to see in the world. Like Paul, you can become an inclusive leader starting right now, by doing the things you know are the right things to do. Whatever is happening in your team right now, this is your team, your career, and it's not going to change on its own. You can become an inclusive leader. Change starts with you. One small act of inclusion can change your day, your team, and maybe even your entire organization. Yes, your actions as an inclusive leader can change your organization. The very fact that you are reading this book demonstrates that you want to be the change, and you want to be an inclusive leader. It's your decision to start this leadership journey. Change can start with you. Start it right now.

One small
act of inclusion
can change your day,
your team, and maybe
even your entire
organization.

RESOURCES

Many of the leaders and HR professionals that I work with in my workshops and training programs ask me what types of tools and resources would best support an inclusive and diverse workplace. Before sharing some practical resources and tools that you can use to boost inclusion and diversity in your organization, I want to be very clear: inclusion is a journey and requires work each day of the year, and inclusive leaders will never be finished with their job. An inclusive workplace requires daily work in learning and listening. It goes beyond completing questionnaires and assessments. As a special bonus resource, you can download your free copy of the ebook "7 Deadly Mistakes to Avoid with Diversity Programmes" by visiting https://www.inspired-human.com/ebook-7-mistakes-to-avoid.

APPENDIX 1

SELF-ASSESSMENT QUESTIONNAIRE

This self-assessment tool is designed to explore individual cultural competence. Its purpose is to help you to consider your awareness in your interactions with others. Its goal is to assist you in recognizing what you can do to become more effective in working and living in a diverse environment. Read each entry in the section below and list your score. **This is simply a tool and not a test.** Remember that cultural competence is a process, and that learning occurs on a continuum and over a lifetime. Though you are not being asked to show anyone your answers, you may choose to do so. While you complete this assessment, stay in touch with your emotions and remind yourself that learning is a journey.

Answer the following questions with either:
- N = Never
- S = Sometimes/Occasionally
- F = Fairly Often/Pretty Well
- A = Always/Very Well

___ I view human differences as positive and a cause for celebration.

___ I have a clear sense of my own ethnic, cultural, and racial identity.

___ I am aware that in order to learn more about others I need to understand and be prepared to share my own culture.

___ I am aware of my discomfort when I encounter differences in race, color, religion, sexual orientation, language, and ethnicity.

___ I am aware of the assumptions that I hold about people of cultures different from my own.

___ I am aware of my stereotypes as they arise and have developed personal strategies for reducing the harm they cause.

___ I am aware of how my cultural perspective influences my judgment about what are "appropriate," "normal," or "superior" behaviors, values, and communication styles.

___ I accept that in cross-cultural situations there can be uncertainty and that uncertainty can make me anxious. It can also mean that I do not respond appropriately or take the time needed to get more information.

___ I take any opportunity to put myself in places where I can learn about differences and create relationships.

___ If I am a white person working with a person of color, I understand that I will likely be perceived as a person with power and racial privilege, and that I may not be seen as "unbiased" or as an ally.

Reflection

At the end of this exercise, add up the number of times you have answered either "Never," "Sometimes/Occasionally," "Fairly Often/Pretty Well," "Always/Very Well." Multiple the number of times you have checked the columns by: Never x 1, Sometimes/Occasionally x 2, Fairly Often/Pretty Well x 3, Always/Very Well x 4 . The more points you have, the more culturally competent you are becoming.

APPENDIX 2

ORGANIZATION DIVERSITY AND INCLUSION ASSESSMENT

This organizational diversity and inclusion assessment will help you better understand where the gaps are in your organization and where you should prioritize your diversity and inclusion efforts.

Please answer the following questions as honestly as possible, using the 1 to 10 ranking, where 1 = not at all and 10 = extremely. Please add explanations for each question to provide as much context as possible.

List score 1 to 10 for each question

Workforce Composition

___ How diversified is your workforce composition?

___ How much does your organization prioritize having a diverse workforce?

___ How well is your organization doing in retaining minorities in the workforce?

Explanation:

Diversity Standards, Policy, Funding, and Evaluation Process

___ How would you rank your organization's efforts to implement an inclusive environment?

___ How strong (if at all) is your organization's strategic plan to reflect any commitment to diversity, including funding allocated to diversity and the evaluation process to determine how diversity is implemented or measured?

Explanation:

Diverse Workforce in Leadership Roles

___ How diversified is your organization's leadership team?

Explanation:

Professional Development for a Diverse Workforce

___ How much of a business priority is the recruitment, retention, and promotion of diverse populations?

___ How strongly/effectively is diversity implemented as a professional development component for the staff?

Explanation:

Internal Leadership Support

___ How powerful is the person (if any) leading the diversity and inclusion efforts? (1 = individual contributor to 10 = SVP reporting to CEO)

Explanation:

Diverse Supplier Component

___ How important is the diverse vendor component (prioritizing diversified vendors) to your organization?

Explanation:

Finances

___ How strong is your organization financially?

Explanation:

Leadership Accountability

___ How strong (if any) are the accountability standards to measure failures or successes on diversity and inclusion?

Explanation:

Disproportionality Index Analysis

___ Do performance reviews look at diversity standards including recruitment and retention of diverse employees for all the employees? (yes or no)

Explanation:

Make a list of your organization's last ten promotions. How diverse do you consider them in terms of gender, ethnicity, and background?

Make a list of your organization's last ten hires. How diverse do you consider them in terms of gender, ethnicity, and background?

If you haven't made enough recent promotions or hires to know, think about your last several all-hands meetings and whose efforts you've acknowledged and think about the last raises and bonuses you've allocated. Are you distributing rewards and recognition in a way that acknowledges a wide-ranging set of contributions?

Think about the last five people to leave your organization. Do you notice any commonality in their circumstances or background?

~~~

Once you have completed this questionnaire, take a moment to analyze your answers. Identify the gaps and make a list of all the areas where you need to improve. Once you have done that, order your list of areas of improvement by priority, ranging from the most important one to the least important one. Then, make a plan to address each area, including the following:

- Who will need to be involved in the plan?

- When you will need to start?

- What specific goals do you desire to meet?

- What will be your timeline to achieve the stated goals?

- What resources will you need?

- What will be your budget requirements?

- What data you will need to start with and then to track?

- How you will achieve each goal?

Share your plans with all the relevant stakeholders

within your organization and create a calendar with regular meetings with the relevant stakeholders to track progress.

APPENDIX 3

ENGAGEMENT SURVEY QUESTIONNAIRE

Employee engagement surveys are a great way to assess your employee engagement, which gives you a great insight into how inclusive your organization really is. When I work with organizations on diversity and inclusion programs, I often advise leaders to filter employee engagement survey results, for example, by geography, department, team, gender, ethnicity, and age.

The organizations I work with are often surprised to see the significant difference of engagement from one team to another. One employer in particular, after breaking down employee engagement results by team, noticed that one team in particular had exceptionally low employee engagement results. They started digging into it and interviewing team members. Their research revealed that one manager in particular was causing very low employee morale, including employee sick days, absenteeism, and poor performance overall. They fired the manager and started quickly noticing

163

better team performance, lower absenteeism, and even increased collaboration and innovation from that team.

It is important that you run regular employee engagement surveys and that you filter the results as mentioned in the previous paragraph to really understand how each group is feeling in regard to your organization. Below is an example of an employee engagement survey questionnaire that you can use in your own organization:

ENGAGEMENT QUESTIONNAIRE

Score each statement 1 to 10 with 10 being the highest score.

___ I'm proud to work for {INSERT COMPANY NAME}. (1 to 10)

___ I would recommend {INSERT COMPANY NAME} as a great place to work. (1 to 10)

___ I rarely think about looking for a job at another company. (1 to 10)

___ I see myself still working at {INSERT COMPANY NAME} in two years' time. (1 to 10)

___{INSERT COMPANY NAME} motivates me to go beyond what I would in a similar role elsewhere. (1 to 10)

ABOUT THE AUTHOR

Perrine Farque is the founder of Inspired Human and is a well-known diversity, inclusion, and leadership expert and consultant. Perrine drove the strategy at leading companies including Facebook, PagerDuty, Pivotal, Nlyte Software, and AvePoint for over a decade. During her career, Perrine managed many teams and worked across multi-cultural groups, and she experienced first-hand what makes teams and organizations succeed: building truly inclusive and diverse teams.

Perrine is an inspiring keynote speaker, author, and inclusion and diversity expert who empowers leaders to leverage diversity as their competitive advantage. Perrine was nominated in the Top 50 Most Influential Women in UK Tech by Computer Weekly and is also a judge at the Diversity in Tech awards. She has been featured as a keynote speaker at many well-established industry conferences including Dublin Tech Summit and IBM's Cascon X Evoke. Perrine is also a frequent contributor in a number of publications including Startup Nation, DiversityQ, Fair Play Talks, and many more.

Perrine has trained many organizations on how to create diverse and inclusive teams to grow their business. She is passionate about educating business leaders to think of diversity and inclusion as their top priority because it is the most important competitive advantage. Perrine's work has been brought into workplaces, institutions, communities, and events around the world, both live and virtually, for those seeking to create an inclusive and diverse environment. Find out more about Perrine at www.inspired-human.com. Get your free copy of the ebook "7 Deadly Mistakes to Avoid with Diversity Programmes" by visiting: https://www.inspired-human.com/ebook-7-mistakes-to-avoid.

LINKEDIN
https://www.linkedin.com/in/perrinefarque/

TWITTER
https://twitter.com/PerrineFarqueUK

FACEBOOK
https://www.facebook.com/PerrineFarque

INSTAGRAM
https://www.instagram.com/perrinefarqueofficial/

YOUTUBE
https://www.youtube.com/channel/UCmYKgD9mNq80PJshb8PZjsg

Printed in Great Britain
by Amazon

36916013R00106